soft toys
TO SEW

All our soft toy patterns are graded so that you can choose a pattern that is just right for you to make.

   for beginners

    for average skills

     for the experienced

Craft Editor: Tonia Todman
Editor: Judy Poulos
Assistant Craft Editor: Sally Pereira
Editorial Co-ordinator: Margaret Kelly
Editorial Assistant: Marian Broderick
Sewing Assistant: Sophie Levitt

Artists: Carol Dunn and Martina Oprey
Photography: Andrew Elton
Design: Margie Mulray
Cover: Amanda Westwood
Artwork: Barbara Martusewicz
Production: Sheridan Carter

Publisher: Philippa Sandall

Family Circle is a registered trademark ® of
IPC Magazines Limited
Published by J. B. Fairfax Press by arrangement
with IPC Magazines Limited
© J. B. Fairfax Press Pty Limited, 1990
Typeset by Adtype, Sydney
Printed by Toppan Printing Co, Hong Kong
Distributed by J. B. Fairfax Press Ltd
9 Trinity Centre, Park Farm Estate
Wellingborough, Northants
Ph: (0933) 402330 Fax: (0933) 402234

Soft Toys To Sew
ISBN 1 86343 001 6

The publishers would like to thank the following
people who assisted in the production of this
book:
Home Yardage, Australia, for supplying all
our fabrics and laces; Bernina and Pfaff,
Australia, who provided sewing machines and
Belinda's Corner Shop, Sydney, Australia, where
we photographed the toys.

Offray provided all our ribbons

UNDER NEW E.C. REGULATIONS TOYS
SHOULD NOT BE MADE FOR RESALE.

METRIC/IMPERIAL CONVERSION CHART

METRIC	INCHES
2 mm	1/16
6 mm	1/4
1 cm	3/8
2.5 cm	1
5 cm	2
30 cm	12
91 cm	36

CONTENTS

SOFT TOYS TO SEW

Cuddly and appealing, soft toys are a favourite with children of all ages. The wonder of these delightful toys is that they begin as playmates but become friends, confidantes and lifelong companions.

In this book you will find a treasury of all-time favourite soft toys to make, from tiny clutch toys for baby to an elegant family of beautifully dressed mice. There are fairytale characters, a traditional rag doll, elephants to cuddle and a bunny backpack for transporting treasures.

There are toys suitable for everyone to sew from the beginner to the expert. Each project has been graded so you can see at a glance whether it's a simple one or one that requires a little patience for a perfect result.

Making these lovely soft toys requires no special skills or fancy equipment. Many of them can be made entirely by hand in a few hours. In fact felt toys of all kinds can be made by hand using a simple blanket stitch. You don't even need a sewing machine!

PRACTICAL BEGINNINGS

This practical introduction discusses fabrics, sewing techniques, patterns and stuffing, and includes plenty of hints and time saving tips for beginners and experienced sewers.

Soft toys can be made from just about any fabric providing it has sufficient strength to cope with firm stuffing and years of wear, tear, love and devotion. Toys which will be handled and dropped and thrown will need to be made from spongeable fabric. Avoid fabrics that fray easily. If you have no choice remember to allow wider seam allowances and zigzag or overlock seams for extra strength. Try also to avoid very bold patterns of stripes and checks for small toys. Use our Fabric Chart (on pages 8-9) to help choose the right materials.

Some pattern pieces, particularly clothing pieces, are interfaced to give added body or shape. In this book we have used fusible or iron-on interfacing which is readily available.

The way you stuff a soft toy is very important as it is this which gives the toy its cuddly feel and appearance.

When stuffing the toys it is best to get it right the first time. Correcting a badly stuffed toy can be quite difficult. Before you begin, tease the fibres or foam into small portions. Push them one at a time into the furthest corners of the toy and work back towards the opening. Use a stuffing stick to ram the material firmly into the hard-to-get-at corners. Mould the toy as you go, making sure there are no gaps. Check the feel of the stuffing and adjust it to be more or less firm depending on the toy. It is a good idea to leave the stuffed toy to settle for a while before closing it up.

It is important to use the correct amount of stuffing in your toy. Too little, and it will look sad and rather shapeless, and won't sit or stand properly. Too much and it will be too hard, not very cuddly and may even burst its seams.

EQUIPMENT

Making soft toys requires no special equipment other than that usually found in a home sewing basket or kitchen cupboard. As well as sewing equipment you will also need sharp pencils, a soft rubber, a tape measure, ruler, cardboard and tracing paper to trace and enlarge the patterns. It is a good idea to assemble all your equipment before you begin.

♥ *Scissors:* Ideally you should have two pairs of sharp scissors – one for cutting out the paper pattern and one for the fabric. A small pair of pointed embroidery scissors can also be useful for the fiddly bits but is not essential. A pair of pinking shears is a bonus when preparing trims and decorations.

♥ *Pins:* Any strong, extra long pins are quite suitable. You may find glass-headed pins or patchworker's T-shaped pins a little easier to use.

♥ *Needles:* You will need a selection of needles suitable for different purposes. For example, crewel-eyed needles for embroidery and extra long needles for attaching limbs and eyes. A curved needle can be useful if you feel comfortable using one.

The most important thing to remember is that all your needles, including sewing machine needles, should be very strong.

♥ *Thread:* A variety of threads will be useful to have on hand when you begin. For attaching limbs and heads and closing holes left for stuffing you will need an especially strong thread. Buttonhole thread, particularly the waxed variety, is ideal for this purpose. If you are unable to buy waxed buttonhole thread it is quite a simple matter to wax your own by running it across beeswax or a white candle.

Any thread can be used to embroider faces as long as it gives the desired effect. In this book we have used wool, stranded cotton and even strands of silk.

Sew seams with a thread colour matched to the fabric and containing some man-made fibre for stretch. Colour matching is quite important because some seams will show when the toy is stuffed. If you are not able to match the colour choose a slightly lighter shade.

♥ *Stuffing Stick:* This can be any long thin tool suitable for turning toys right side out and for ramming stuffing into tight corners.

Chopsticks, the blunt end of a knitting needle or even a screwdriver can be used. A wonderful tool for stuffing toys is the end of a pencil wrapped with sticky tape, sticky side out. The stuffing will stick to the tape and be carried easily to the far corners. Take care not

to damage the fabric when using sharp objects such as these.

♥ *Glue:* Keep a good quality craft glue on hand. It should be quick-drying, stainless and remain flexible when dry. A PVA clear drying glue, hot melt glue gun or clear stainless glue are all ideal.

♥ *Hole Punch:* A hole punch is very useful for cutting out tiny felt dots for pupils of eyes or for decorative trimming, such as we have used on our hippo's collar.

♥ *Compass:* You will need some help with marking and cutting out circles. A compass or even the lip of a cup or saucer will do very well.

♥ *Sewing Machine:* Not only useful for sewing toys but also embroidering dolls' clothes.

USING THE PATTERNS

The patterns have been reduced to fit our page. They have been drawn on a squared grid where each square is 2.5 cm x 2.5 cm (1" x 1"). To enlarge these patterns to their actual size follow these simple steps:

1 Tape or pin a sheet of firm tracing paper over the grid sheet provided. Drawing your patterns on tracing paper in this way will enable you to use your grid sheet over and over again.

2 With a sharp, soft pencil begin drawing at a point where the pattern line coincides with the intersection of four squares. Make a dot at this point.

3   Work your way carefully around each pattern piece making a dot at each point where the pattern line intersects with a line of the grid.

4   Now simply join up the dots. Keep a soft rubber handy for any little slips or squiggles.

5   Transfer all symbols and markings to each pattern piece.

6   Label and cut out each pattern piece. Take care to transfer all symbols and markings.

Some patterns have been divided to fit on the page. After tracing, tape adjoining edges together without overlapping.

JOINING AND STITCHING

Most of our soft toys are machine sewn on the inside with seam allowances as given. These seams need to be very strong to withstand the pressure of stuffing and years of happy play. Tails, limbs and heads should be especially secure. Pressure points and tight corners should be reinforced with an extra row of stitching. Take care also to secure the beginning and end of each seam. Some toys may be easier to handle if basted first, especially if you are a beginner.

Any felt toy can also be hand-sewn using a strong thread, doubled, and a simple backstitch. Where the seam is to be visible on the outside, pattern pieces can be joined using doubled thread and buttonhole stitch.

Remember that for a smooth finish it is essential to trim and clip all seam allowances before a toy is turned right side out.

Ladder stitch is the most suitable for closing the opening after the toy has been stuffed. This gives a very secure closure and one that is almost invisible when complete. Beginning at one end of the opening, take a few stitches as shown, alternating right to left with left to right stitches (see diagram). Pull up the thread quite tightly to close that part of the hole already stitched. Continue in this way until the entire hole is closed. Fasten threads off very securely.

MAKING FACES

Embroidering or sewing on the features is the final important step in making your soft toy. How you decorate the face will determine the personality and expression.

There are a number of choices you can make for each facial feature. You will find some specific tips on decorating a teddy bear, a doll or even a hippo alongside the particular pattern but here are some general tips to follow.

You should choose the features, particularly the eyes, best suited to the type of toy you have chosen. The eyes can be embroidered on, made from beads, buttons or felt, or you can purchase safety-lock eyes from your craft shop. Generally the safest eyes for small childrens' toys, that you can make yourself, are embroidered or felt ones. If you do use buttons or beads be certain to attach them very well using either dental floss or waxed buttonhole thread. Position the eyes very carefully. Wide apart eyes give a look of innocence or move them closer together for a stern look.

Contouring the eye socket before attaching the eyes gives a realistic shape to the face. This can be done quite simply by stitching across from one eye socket, through the head to the other side and pulling up the threads very tightly.

Mouths and noses can be embroidered in stem stitch, chain stitch or satin stitch or glued on in felt. (see diagrams). Again choose the shape, style and colour to suit your toy and give it the expression you are looking for.

Features can also be painted on using fabric paints, crayons or even your own powder blusher for a doll's cheeks.

Experiment with all these ideas and some of your own until you find just the right combination for your soft toy.

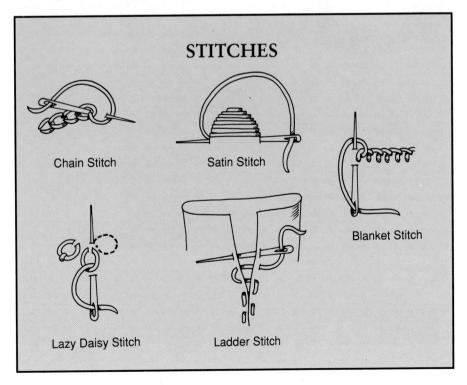

STITCHES

Chain Stitch

Satin Stitch

Blanket Stitch

Lazy Daisy Stitch

Ladder Stitch

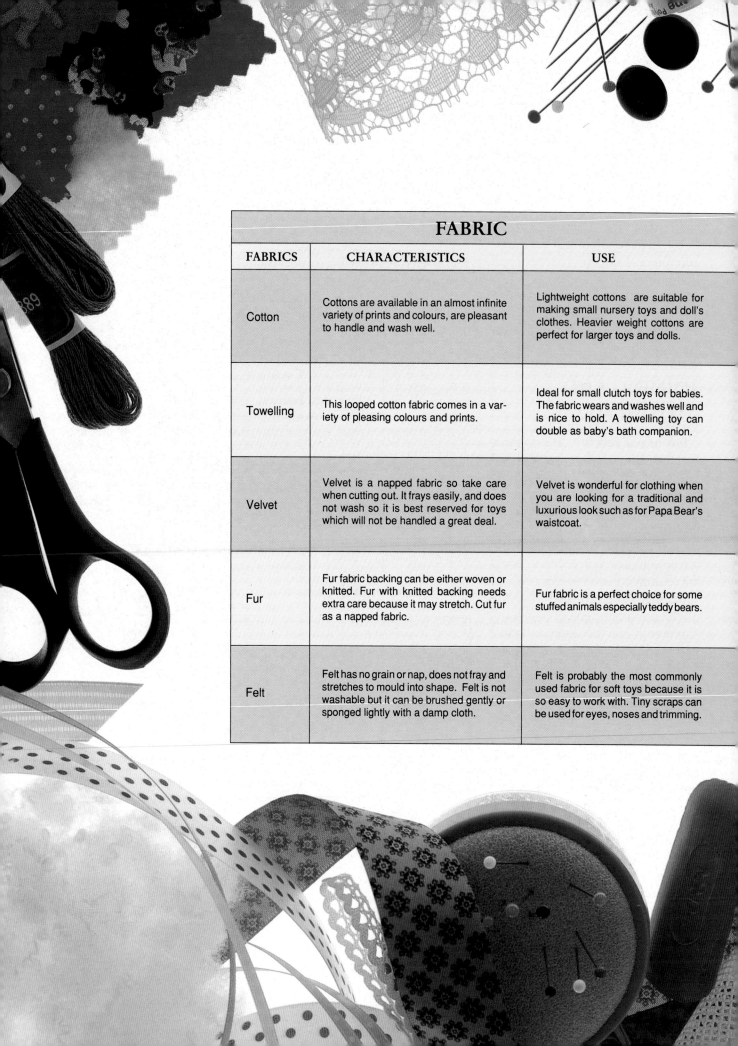

FABRIC

FABRICS	CHARACTERISTICS	USE
Cotton	Cottons are available in an almost infinite variety of prints and colours, are pleasant to handle and wash well.	Lightweight cottons are suitable for making small nursery toys and doll's clothes. Heavier weight cottons are perfect for larger toys and dolls.
Towelling	This looped cotton fabric comes in a variety of pleasing colours and prints.	Ideal for small clutch toys for babies. The fabric wears and washes well and is nice to hold. A towelling toy can double as baby's bath companion.
Velvet	Velvet is a napped fabric so take care when cutting out. It frays easily, and does not wash so it is best reserved for toys which will not be handled a great deal.	Velvet is wonderful for clothing when you are looking for a traditional and luxurious look such as for Papa Bear's waistcoat.
Fur	Fur fabric backing can be either woven or knitted. Fur with knitted backing needs extra care because it may stretch. Cut fur as a napped fabric.	Fur fabric is a perfect choice for some stuffed animals especially teddy bears.
Felt	Felt has no grain or nap, does not fray and stretches to mould into shape. Felt is not washable but it can be brushed gently or sponged lightly with a damp cloth.	Felt is probably the most commonly used fabric for soft toys because it is so easy to work with. Tiny scraps can be used for eyes, noses and trimming.

STUFFING

FABRICS	CHARACTERISTICS	WASHABLE?
Polyester Fibre	This ideal stuffing material is lightweight and very easy to use. Always choose polyester fibre when the weight of a toy is important such as for backpacks or babies' toys.	Yes
Kapok	Kapok is a very traditional and relatively inexpensive material. These days, however, it can be quite difficult to find. Kapok is also fairly awkward to use and can be quite messy.	No
Foam Crumbs	Foam is quite satisfactory for stuffing and relatively inexpensive. It can be difficult to achieve a smooth look with foam. It also tends to collect dust which might be a problem if a child is allergic.	Yes
Odds and Ends	Many toys can be stuffed with scraps of soft fabric or strips of old stockings. These have the obvious cost advantage but can produce a very heavy and sometimes lumpy toy.	No

BEAR ESSENTIALS

eautiful bears have a special place in all our hearts. The Three Bears are firm favourites with young and old. Any child would enjoy the security and comfort of snuggling down to sleep with cuddly Benjamin Bear.

Any strong fabric can be used to make a bear and he doesn't have to be brown! Experiment with different fabrics and colours. Try combining cotton prints for a patchwork bear or trimming a plain brown felt bear with tartan paws and waistcoat. For a truly bear-like bear choose a fur fabric. You will be rewarded for the additional cost and work involved.

How much stuffing you use will depend on whether you want your bear to sit unaided, in which case you should stuff it very firmly, or whether you want a soft and cuddly teddy which will need much less stuffing.

A bear's facial expression comes from the position and style of his features. Mouths and noses are generally embroidered on when the toy is complete. To get the smile just right, mark out the position with pins. Experiment until you are pleased with the result then wind wool around the pins. Stitch the wool into place. Teddy bears generally have button eyes or, if you prefer, safety-lock eyes purchased from a craft shop. Personalise your very special bear by embroidering his name, or yours, and the date on his back. In years to come it will be a wonderful family heirloom.

The three bears

For a truly traditional teddy, we chose a truly traditional tale. Imagine the bedtime fun of acting out the story of The Three Bears with a real family of bears like these.

We chose wool fabric for our bears and dressed Papa Bear in velvet adding a serious touch with his fine wire spectacles. Mama Bear is dressed just right for a walk in the woods before breakfast. And little children will find it easy to change Baby Bear's nappy.

DIMENSIONS
Papa Bear: 44 cm tall; Mama Bear: 36 cm tall; Baby Bear: 29 cm tall

MATERIALS
Bears
Papa Bear: 40 cm wool fabric or felt;
Mama Bear: 35 cm wool fabric or felt;
Baby Bear: 25 cm wool fabric or felt.
For each bear you will need two buttons for eyes; polyester fibre for stuffing; scraps of felt or velvet for foot pads and paws; four 20 mm buttons for attaching limbs; sewing thread; elastic; embroidery thread for decorating face.

Clothes
Papa Bear's vest: 20 cm velvet; 20 cm lining; three buttons; small buckle; 2.5 cm velvet ribbon; 20 cm flexible but firm wire for spectacles.

Mama Bear's dress: 20 cm of 115 cm wide cotton fabric; one button; 1.7 m gathered lace for trim.
Baby Bear's nappy: 25 cm square of towelling, hemmed; ribbon.

PATTERN
All three bears are made following the same instructions but in different sizes. Cut out pattern pieces as directed. 1 cm seam allowed all around each pattern piece.
Cut to size: Mama bear's skirt 10 cm x 110 cm; waistband 5 cm x 45 cm; straps 25 cm x 5 cm (cut 2); ruffles 10 cm x 33 cm (cut 2).

STEP-BY-STEP
Clip all curved seam allowances for ease. Join all pieces together with right sides facing.

Bears

1   Sew darts in side head sections. Join head sections at chin, between A and C. Pin and baste centre head section to side sections from B to C, taking care to centre nose at C. You may need to ease this seam a little. Stitch. Turn in 1 cm around neck edge. Baste with small stitches. Stuff head firmly.

2   Place paw pieces onto arms at points Z and Y with right sides facing. Stitch. Sew arm sections together leaving an opening for turning.

3   Sew leg sections together leaving an opening for turning. Sew foot pad to foot matching points F and B. Clip seam allowance for ease. Reinforce instep area of leg. Snip into curve. Turn arms and legs right side out. Stuff firmly. Close openings by hand.

4   Sew fronts to backs at side seams. Matching points E, join sewn body pieces together by stitching from front neck, down centre front through E and around to D. Stuff body firmly.

5   Place ear sections together with right sides facing. Stitch around curved edges. Clip seam. Turn and press. Turn in approx 1 cm at lower raw edges. Baste.

6   To attach limbs, thread a length of elastic through eyes of a 20 mm button. Make a small slit on inner surface of arms and legs at markings. Push button well into limb through this slit, enclosing it with stuffing. Sew up opening enclosing button but keeping elastic free. Thread a long, crewel-eyed needle with this elastic and pass it through body at points marked and out other side. Unthread elastic and pass end through holes of another button. Push this second button into a slit in limb as before. Sew up slit. Thread elastic onto needle again and push back through body as before. Unthread elastic and pull up very firmly, bringing limbs close to body. Tie ends of elastic together very securely, trim ends and push knot into body if possible. Arms and legs should rotate and move smoothly.

7   Pin head to body so that A matches with centre front seam. If necessary add extra filling to neck area. Neatly and firmly stitch head to body.

8   Embroider features onto face as shown using satin stitch for nose and long straight stitches for mouth. Sew eyes to head bringing thread out at ear points. Pull thread slightly to add contour to face. Stitch between eyes pulling thread to contour face as before. Attach ears as invisibly as possible.

Papa Bear's Vest

1   Make darts in front and back of vest and lining sections.

2   Sew fronts to back at shoulders.

3   Place vest and lining with right sides together and matching raw edges. Stitch from side front around front opening edges and neckline. Stitch across lower back edge. Turn right side out and press.

4   Cut two strips from scrap fabric, each 7 cm x 6 cm. Fold in half lengthways with right sides together. Stitch ends and turn. Stitch raw edge along pocket line with folded edge of flap pointing towards shoulder. Fold flaps down. Stitch ends down through all thicknesses.

5   Cut two strips from scrap velvet fabric each 6 cm x 12 cm. Fold lengthways with right sides together. Stitch along one short and long edge for each strip. Turn and press. Fold under raw edge and stitch onto markings at back vest. Attach buckle.

6   Sew vest side seams.

7   Make three buttonholes in front vest. Sew on buttons.

8   Fold wire into shape for spectacles as shown.

9   Tie bow around neck.

Mama Bear's Dress

1   Gather one long edge of skirt. Stitch lace around other edge. Make three small pintucks above lace along skirt hem. Turn in 2 cm on skirt centre back edges.

2   Measure bear's waist. Gather skirt to this measurement plus 4 cm. Place right side of waistband on wrong side of skirt. Stitch. Fold waistband with right sides facing. Sew short ends. Turn waistband and fold over right side of skirt. Turn in raw edge. Stitch through all thicknesses.

3   Fold ruffle with wrong sides facing. Gather raw edges. Pin lace over gathering stitches. Place straps onto ruffles with right side facing and raw edges even. Stitch. Press strap flat. Pin straps to skirt centre front at an angle to pass neatly over shoulders. Stitch. Attach straps to inside back waistband on either side of back opening.

4   Make buttonhole and sew button on back waistband.

Baby Bear

Fold nappy and pin on bear. Tie bow around neck.

✂ **H I N T** ✂

Finish all your seams well and make sure they are strong enough to cope with years of boisterous play. Backstitch at the beginning and end of each seam or tie threads off very carefully to ensure that seams do not unravel.

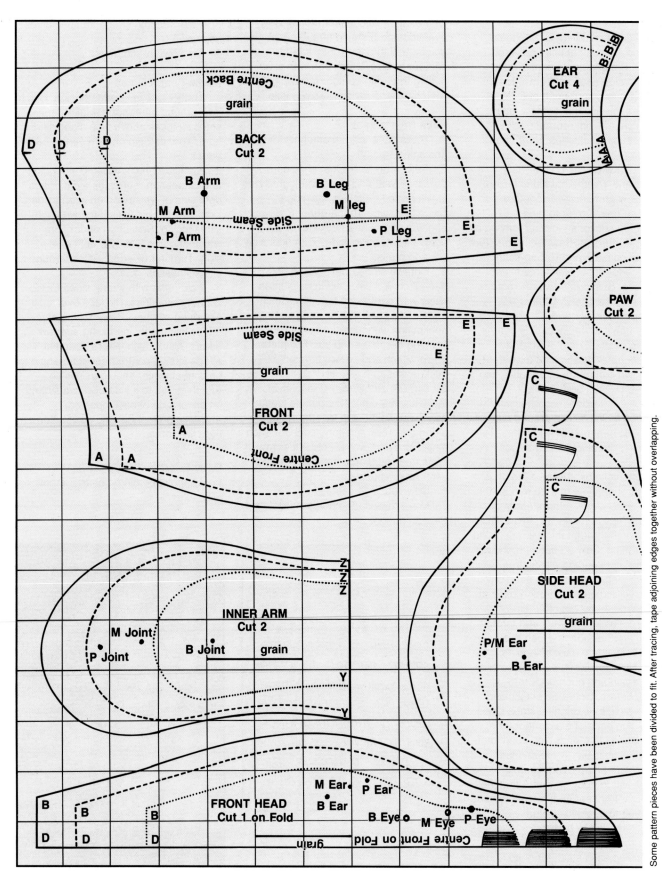

Some pattern pieces have been divided to fit. After tracing, tape adjoining edges together without overlapping.

Each square is 2.5 cm x 2.5 cm.   **KEY P - Papa Bear M - Mama Bear B - Baby Bear — grainline.**

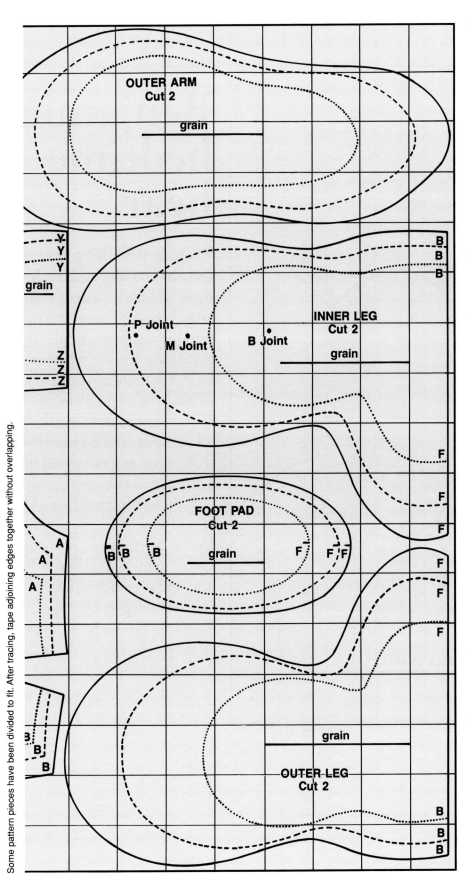

OUTER ARM
Cut 2

grain

Y
Y
Y

grain

Z
Z
Z

P Joint
M Joint
B Joint

INNER LEG
Cut 2

grain

B
B
B

F
F
F

FOOT PAD
Cut 2

grain

A
A
A

B B B

F F F

F

F

F

F

B
B
B

grain

OUTER LEG
Cut 2

B
B
B

Some pattern pieces have been divided to fit. After tracing, tape adjoining edges together without overlapping.

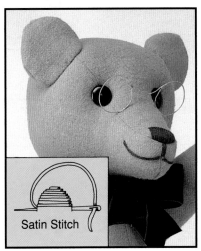

See over for
Papa's Vest

Satin Stitch

THE 3 BEARS

Benjamin, bedtime bear

There is something very special about a big, cuddly, furry bear. We chose a rich chocolatey brown for our Benjamin, but this design would also look great as a snowy white polar bear. There are no special tricks of the trade when sewing fur fabric except to keep the fur all running in the same direction – just as you would with a napped fabric.

We think Benjamin is a very friendly grizzly. He certainly looks as though he would enjoy games, bedtime stories and hiding under the covers when the lights go out.

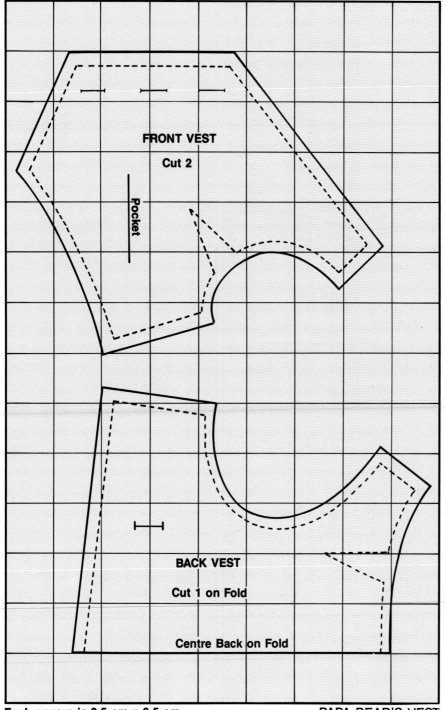

FRONT VEST

Cut 2

Pocket

BACK VEST

Cut 1 on Fold

Centre Back on Fold

Each square is 2.5 cm x 2.5 cm.

PAPA BEAR'S VEST

DIMENSIONS
39 cm high when seated

MATERIALS
70 cm of 140 cm wide fur fabric; two shiny black 1.5 cm shank buttons for eyes; 1.1 m of 1.5 cm wide satin ribbon for bow; scrap of plain cotton fabric for snout lining; embroidery thread for decorating face.

PATTERN
Cut out pattern pieces as directed.
1 cm seam allowed around all pattern pieces.

STEP-BY-STEP
Clip all curved seam allowances for ease. Join all pieces together with right sides facing.

HINT: Fur fabric is much easier to handle if you pin all seams before you sew with long, glass-headed pins placed across the seam line at right angles. After sewing, use a pin to tease out fibres caught in the seam. You will find this quite effectively covers the stitching and gives a 'seam-free' result.

1 Sew dart in front leg. Join front leg to upper foot along seam A.
2 Join front leg to back leg along seam B and along seam C to centre back.
3 Join under foot to completed leg along circular seam D–E. Repeat for other leg.
4 Sew darts in back body. Join front body sections to back body along seam F. Join centre front body seam.
5 Sew tail sections together. Clip seam, turn. Stuff tail lightly and attach to body matching centre back symbols.
6 Join both legs to body along seams G, H and I.
7 Sew paws to lower arm pieces along seam J. Sew arm sections together along K and L for both arms. Join arms to body along M, N and O.
8 Stuff body firmly. Using buttonhole or other strong thread, gather neck edge slightly and secure.
9 Make darts in side head sections. Join front head to side head sections.
10 Sew ear sections together. Clip seam and turn. Sew ears to side head sections along Q, matching notches. Sew complete front head to back head.

✄ HINT ✄
Oil your sewing machine well while sewing soft toys. Remember it is having to cope with multiple layers of very thick materials. You should use thicker than usual machine needles and stitch more slowly when sewing thick fabric or felt.

11 Sew dart in lower snout. Join to upper snout along seam R. Join snout to front head along S. Sew snout lining to snout leaving an opening at lower edge for stuffing. Stuff snout very firmly. Close opening.
12 Stuff head firmly. Gather neck edge as before.
13 Contour eye sockets by threading a long needle with very strong thread and stitching from one eye socket through the head to other side. Attach eyes very securely.
14 Embroider nose in satin stitch and mouth with long straight stitches.
15 Handsew head to body, matching centre fronts and centre backs.
16 Trim neck with bow.

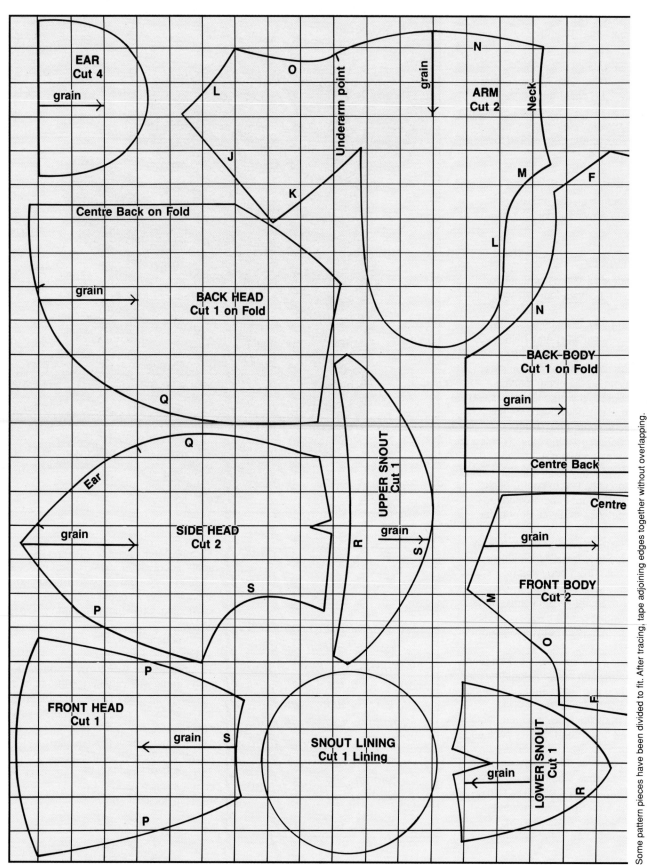

EAR Cut 4
grain

BACK HEAD Cut 1 on Fold
Centre Back on Fold
grain

SIDE HEAD Cut 2
Ear
grain
Q
P
S

FRONT HEAD Cut 1
grain
S
P
P

O
L
J
K
Underarm point
grain

ARM Cut 2
N
Neck
M
L
F
N

BACK BODY Cut 1 on Fold
grain
Centre Back
Centre

UPPER SNOUT Cut 1
R
grain
S

FRONT BODY Cut 2
M
O
F

SNOUT LINING Cut 1 Lining

LOWER SNOUT Cut 1
grain
R

Each square is 2.5 cm x 2.5 cm.

Some pattern pieces have been divided to fit. After tracing, tape adjoining edges together without overlapping.

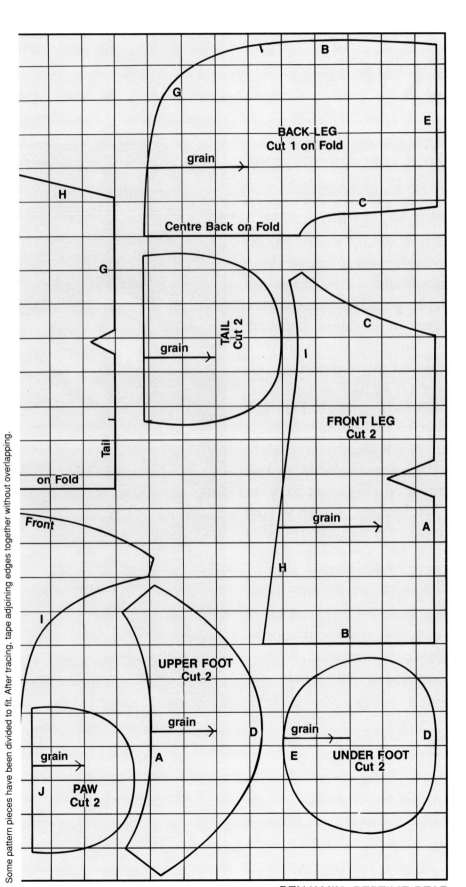

BACK LEG
Cut 1 on Fold

grain →

Centre Back on Fold

B

G

E

H

C

G

grain →

TAIL
Cut 2

Tail

on Fold

Front

I

C

I

FRONT LEG
Cut 2

grain →

A

H

B

UPPER FOOT
Cut 2

grain →

D

A

grain →

E

UNDER FOOT
Cut 2

D

grain →

J

PAW
Cut 2

Some pattern pieces have been divided to fit. After tracing, tape adjoining edges together without overlapping.

BENJAMIN, BEDTIME BEAR

⚞ **H I N T** ⚟

Buttonhole thread or dental floss are both extremely strong. Use to attach eyes and limbs onto toys or to contour faces.

OFF TO THE ZOO

day at the zoo is always fun. Having your own zoo at home makes every day special. All the young zookeeper needs is a little space, a broom, a plastic bucket and some of these favourite zoo animals to look after. We have chosen a pair of elephants, a hippo and a very sweet lion, called Leonard. Elsewhere in this book you will find other appealing animals to add to your collection as time goes by.

We have chosen coloured felt for our zoo animals. Felt is so sturdy and long lasting it will withstand many hours of boisterous play. The wonderful colours of felt lend themselves to some very imaginative effects – such as a lime green hippo. You can, if you prefer, choose quite realistic colours as we have for Eloise the elephant and her baby. Felt has just enough stretch built into the fabric to allow it to take on a lovely rounded shape. Many other strong fabrics also give a pleasing result.

Firm stuffing is very important to keep the detailed shaping of the animals. This is particularly so if the toy is to stand up on its own and not flop over. Take care not to have them too heavy when finished. All these toys are a fair size and should not be too cumbersome for the young keeper to manage.

These animals are meant to be whimsical and fun. A baby elephant in floral rompers or a hippo in a shocking pink, polka dot collar may be somewhat incongruous but are very appealing. Hats are another wonderful trimming idea. Facial expressions and friendly smiles are very important. Experiment with different ways of decorating the faces until you find one that pleases you. Try embroidered faces or glued on felt shapes which can vary greatly in size and shape. You will see how we have caricatured the hippo's bulging eyes by using little balls of stuffed felt while the elephant's slightly bashful look is indicated with rows of luxuriant lashes.

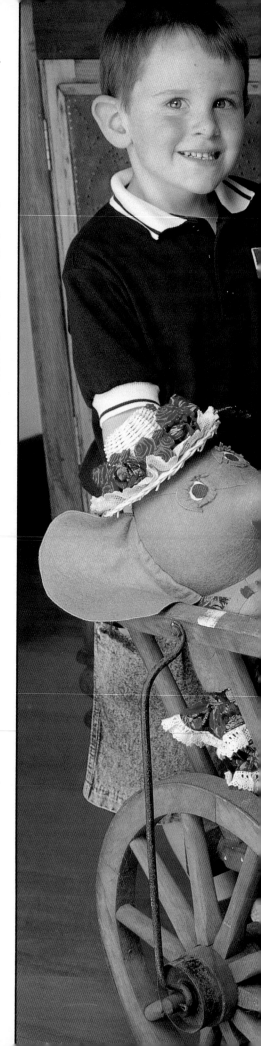

Hortense the hippo

A hippo may seem rather unusual for a cuddly toy, but we found the design for Hortense quite irresistible. Since she is made of felt, she should certainly never, ever wallow in the mud or get wet. In fact, we feel that Hortense is a very particular hippopotamus – the sort who loves cuddles, warm sunshine, soft beds and sweet music. She would definitely hate windy days, brussels sprouts and muddy puddles.

The green and pink polka dot collar seemed like the perfect finishing touch. You might like to go a step further and add a matching pink polka dot parasol?

DIMENSIONS
39 cm long

MATERIALS
25 cm green felt; pink felt for collar and soles of feet; scraps of white and brown felt for eyes; polyester fibre for stuffing; sewing thread.

PATTERN
Cut pattern pieces out as directed.
6 mm seam allowed around all pattern pieces.
Cut to size: rectangle of felt for tail 8 cm long x 6 cm wide, clipped into eight strips by making 5 cm deep cuts along its length.

STEP-BY-STEP
Clip all curved seam allowances for ease. Join main body sections together using zigzag stitching. These are exposed seams and will be visible when the toy is complete.
1   Make darts in body and underbody as marked.
2   Stitch underbody sections together between 1s and 2s leaving an opening for stuffing.
3   Join underbody to lower body, matching markings and stitching from 3 through 4, 5, 6, 7, 8, 9 to 1.
4   Stitch soles to feet easing to fit as necessary.
5   Stitch two ear sections together. Repeat for other ear.
6   Pin head gusset to body, matching markings and starting at 2 at underbody centre seam. Continue stitching head to gusset over ear area to end at 10. Repeat for other side but do not stop at end of gusset. Continue stitching centre back seam as far as 1. Ease where necessary for smooth seaming.
7   Roll tail tightly. Secure with hand sewing. Stitch unclipped end of tail to hippo above 1.
8   Stuff firmly.
9   Take two white felt circles for eyes, gather around edge and draw up slightly. Stuff lightly. Draw up threads firmly. Flatten backs of eyes and stitch to secure. Stitch or glue eyes to head as marked. Cut pupils from brown felt as shown and glue to eyes with Vs at top.
10 Fold ears as shown. Handsew to head as marked.
11 Cut 2 cm wide strip of felt with pinking shears and secure around neck for collar. Cut 2 rectangles of pink felt with pinking shears, each 6 cm x 11 cm. Glue together. Draw in at centre, using scrap of felt and handsew to form bow. Glue bow to centre back collar. Cover bow and collar with small spots glued on as shown. A paper punch is ideal for cutting out small dots.
12 Stitch on Hortense's smile with chain stitch.

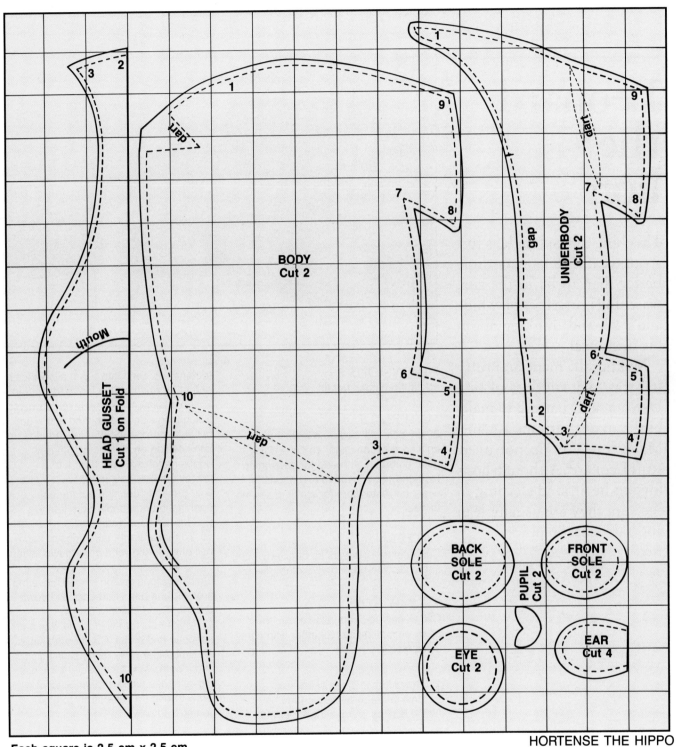

HEAD GUSSET
Cut 1 on Fold

Mouth

BODY
Cut 2

UNDERBODY
Cut 2

gap

dart

BACK SOLE
Cut 2

FRONT SOLE
Cut 2

PUPIL
Cut 2

EYE
Cut 2

EAR
Cut 4

Each square is 2.5 cm x 2.5 cm.

HORTENSE THE HIPPO

Leonard the lion

This king of the jungle is just a pussycat. He likes nothing better than to lie in the sun, watching butterflies play hide and seek and thinking about his next meal.

Making the mane and tufty tail was easy and lots of fun. Use the same pattern to make him a mate, without a mane. Make sure you do not over-stuff Leonard. Although lions love to lie around sleeping in the sun, they are usually lean and rather laconic!

DIMENSIONS
53 cm from nose to tail

MATERIALS
30 cm gold felt; two 50 g balls 8 ply knitting wool, one light and one dark gold; embroidery thread for decorating face and paws; two brown buttons for eyes; polyester fibre for stuffing; sewing thread.

PATTERN
Cut out pattern pieces as directed. 1 cm seam allowed around all pattern pieces.

STEP-BY-STEP
Clip all curved seam allowances for ease. Join all pieces together with right sides facing.

1   Sew darts in sides of body.
2   Join underbody pieces together from L to N leaving an opening for turning.
3   Place ear sections together with right sides facing. Stitch around curved edge. Clip seam, turn and press.
4   Sew chin piece to head gusset, stitching from A to B. Sew other end of chin piece to underbody at Ds.
5   Sew head gusset to side body sections from H to J and K to L.
6   Stitch twice around openings in legs to reinforce. Snip into seam allowances of feet for ease. Stitch foot pads to feet.
7   Fold tail section double lengthways. Stitch long side and pointed end. Turn tail right side out. Stuff firmly. Pin tail into position on side body with raw edges matching. Sew from L to E catching tail as you sew.
8   Turn lion right side out through opening in underbody. Stuff firmly.
9   Sew on eyes and ears.
10 To make mane, take ends of each ball of wool and wind around two fingers 7 or 8 times making loops. Sew each bunch of loops on lion's head, covering area around head and ears and down back to E and chest to Ds.
11 Make tufts for tail in same way and attach to end of tail. Cut through loops.
12 Embroider nose using satin stitch and mouth using long straight stitches. Indicate toes using straight stitches. Draw thread up quite firmly to give contours to paws.

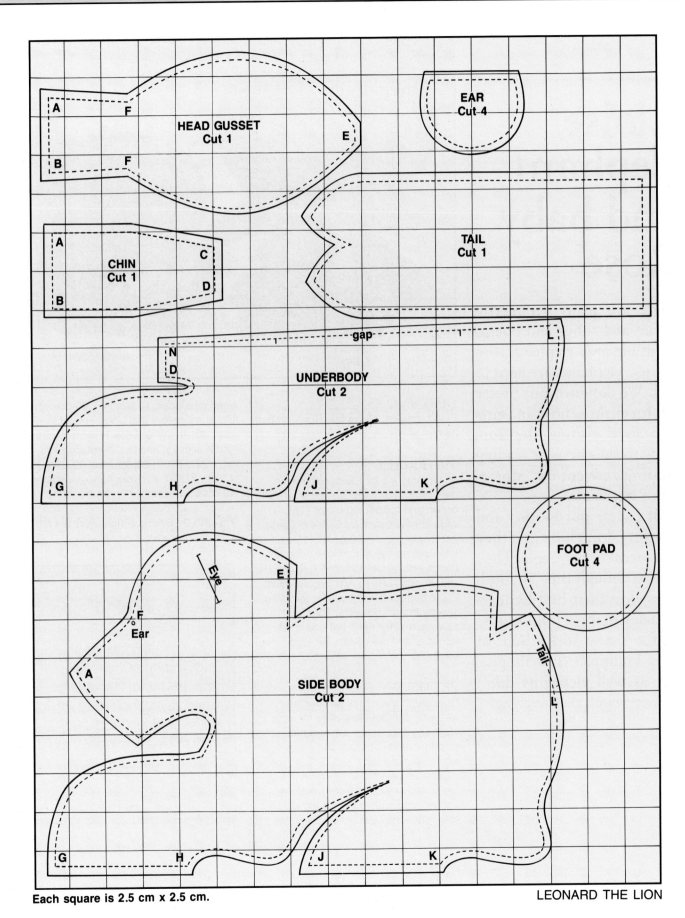

HEAD GUSSET
Cut 1

EAR
Cut 4

CHIN
Cut 1

TAIL
Cut 1

UNDERBODY
Cut 2

gap

FOOT PAD
Cut 4

Eye

Ear

SIDE BODY
Cut 2

Tail

Each square is 2.5 cm x 2.5 cm.

LEONARD THE LION

Eloise elephant and baby Rose

There are many wonderful stories and songs and poems about big grey elephants, but soft toy elephants are hard to find. We designed our pretty pair for all those boys and girls who love visiting the zoo, going to the circus or reading exciting adventure stories about elephants.

Of course our mother and daughter don't look as if they have ever seen a jungle. They look as though they are both dressed in their best bonnets for a day in town followed by far too many sticky buns at Miss Philippa's Tea Shoppe. Just as well elephants don't have to watch their weight!

DIMENSIONS
Eloise, seated: 45 cm tall; Rose, seated: 36 cm tall

MATERIALS
50 cm grey felt for Eloise and 40 cm grey felt for her baby; scraps of white brown and red felt; 60 cm of 115 cm wide printed cotton for Eloise's dress and bloomers and 50 cm of 115 cm wide printed cotton for Rose's rompers; 25 cm iron on interfacing; 1.6 m of 5 mm wide elastic; two 13 mm buttons each; 2.2 m gathered lace each for trimming; sewing thread; polyester fibre for stuffing; a straw doll's hat and small bunch of artificial flowers for each elephant.

PATTERN
Cut pattern pieces out as directed following appropriate outline for each elephant. 1 cm seam allowed around all elephant pattern pieces and 6 mm seam on clothing pieces.
Baby's rompers cut to size: frill 114 cm x 5 cm; pocket band 7.5 cm x 4.5 cm; pocket band interfacing 7.5 cm x 2.25 cm; front band 12.5 cm x 4.5 cm; front band interfacing 12.5 cm x 2.25 cm.
Eloise's pinafore and bloomers cut to size: waistband and ties 114 cm x 4.5 cm; waistband and ties interfacing 114 cm x 2.25 cm; shoulder strap 49 cm x 4.5 cm (cut 2); shoulder strap interfacing 49 cm x 2.25 cm (cut 2); pocket band 7.5 cm x 4.5 cm; pocket band interfacing 7.5 cm x 2.25 cm; pinafore skirt 114 cm x 16 cm (including 1.5 cm hem).

✂ H I N T ✂

Co-ordinating fabrics give a very special look. Keep this in mind especially when selecting fabric for dolls' clothes. Add lashings of lace and ribbon to delight any young lady!

arms to body at straight neck edges matching 11s and 12s.

7   Join upper and under leg sections. Sew legs to body placing 13s on lower body seam.

8   Join head to body matching centre fronts and centre backs.

9   Turn right side out. Stuff firmly. Close opening by hand.

10 Cut two circles from white felt each about 2 cm in diameter but slightly oval-shaped. Cut two circles of brown felt each about 1 cm in diameter. Cut two black ovals for pupils about 8 mm long and 4 mm wide. With double sewing thread stitch from one side of head through stuffing to other side. Pull thread quite firmly to contour eye sockets. Glue layers of eye sections into place.

11 To make eyelashes cut two semi circles each about 6 cm long x 2 cm wide. Clip one side to form lashes. Take care not to clip right through strip but to leave a base for glueing. Curve and glue this section above eye. Make a smaller set of inner lashes in same way and glue under upper lashes covering top of eye. Cut a set of lower lashes about 5 cm long x 2 cm wide. Curve lower lashes and glue butted up to lower edge of white eye section.

12 Cut a wide smile out of crimson felt and glue into place.

13 Cut twelve small red felt finger and toe nails each about 1 cm x 7 mm with curved edges. Glue three to each foot and hand.

Baby's Rompers

1   Iron interfacing onto wrong sides of front, pocket and side bands. Sew pocket band to pocket top, inserting length of lace into seam. Fold pocket band self-facing over to inside. On outside stitch in groove of seam, fixing self-facing in place as you go. Edgestitch top and lower edges of band.

2   Press in 6 mm around curved edge of pocket. Edgestitch pocket to left front rompers as marked.

3   Sew side and crotch seams. Press.

4   Sew lace around edge of frill and lower legs. Press seams towards fabric. Edgestitch to fix in place.

5   Join short ends of frill. Press. Gather top edge of frill. Sew frill 5 cm

STEP-BY-STEP

Neaten all exposed edges. Clip all curved seam allowances for ease. Join all pieces together with right sides facing except for ears. Both elephants are made following the same instructions but in different sizes.

Elephants

1   Sew two ear sections together with wrong sides facing and using zigzag stitching. Matching symbols stitch from 1 through 2 to 3.

2   Join head pieces matching 4s and 5s and continue stitching to end of trunk.

Sew lower head seam from 6 to 7. Clip around end of trunk. Insert tip of trunk.

3   Attach ears to head matching 1 to 4 and 3 to 8.

4   Sew centre back seam of back head sections. Insert this section into back of head matching 8s. Stitch through all thicknesses. Clip seam. Turn.

5   Join body fronts at centre front and backs at centre back, leaving an opening for stuffing. Join front and back at side seams, matching 9s and 10s. Join body sections across lower edge.

6   Join upper arm to under arm around outer edges. Clip seams and turn. Sew

from top edge of rompers, adjusting gathers and placing frill seam at centre back of rompers.

6   Attach front band to rompers as pocket band.

7   Sew side bands to back bands at side seams. Sew side band facings to back band facings at side seams. Press. Sew side and back bands to rompers matching side seams and front edge notches. With right sides together sew band facings to bands. Continue stitching all around straps to front edge notches. Trim and clip seams. Turn straps. Press.

8   Turn facings to inside. On outside stitch in groove of seam, fixing facing into place. Edgestitch all around straps and top edge of band.

9   Make 16 mm buttonhole at end of each strap. Sew buttons on back band as marked.

10 Zigzag 25 cm elastic along marked line on inside of each leg to form frills.

Eloise's Pinafore and Bloomers

1   Iron interfacing onto wrong side of front band, pocket band, shoulder straps and centre 40 cm of waistband.

2   Round off centre back corners of pinafore skirt. Turn in 5 mm along raw edge. Press. Turn in 1 cm again. Press. Stitch hem into place. Stitch again close to edge.

3   Make and trim pocket as for Rose's rompers. Attach pocket to pinafore placing left pocket edge 14 cm from skirt centre front and lower pocket edge 1.5 cm from finished hem of skirt.

4   Gather top edge of pinafore to 40 cm. Attach to centre front waistband. Press waistband self-facing to inside. On outside edgestitch lower edge of waistband, fixing self-facing into place.

5   Turn in seam allowances on ties. Press. Edgestitch all around ties.

6   Attach front band to top edge of pinafore bib in same manner as for Rose's rompers inserting lace into seam as for pocket band.

7   Stitch lace to outside edge of shoulder straps, curving lace away to nothing at back ends of straps. Fold strap self-facings to inside, turn in raw edges and stitch down. Continue stitching all around shoulder straps.

8   Press raw side edges of front bib to outside. Lay shoulder straps on bib with

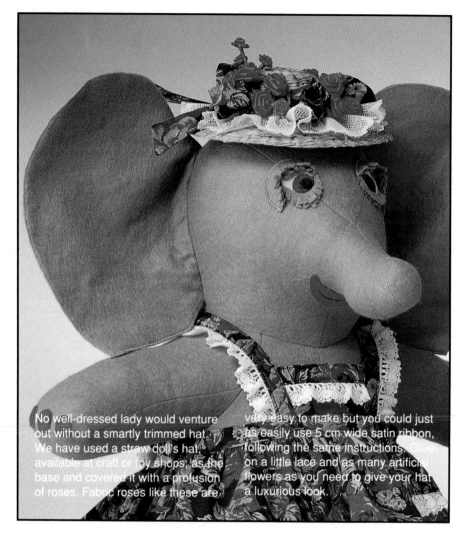

No well-dressed lady would venture out without a smartly trimmed hat. We have used a straw doll's hat, available at craft or toy shops, as the base and covered it with a profusion of roses. Fabric roses like these are very easy to make but you could just as easily use 5 cm wide satin ribbon, following the same instructions. Glue on a little lace and as many artificial flowers as you need to give your hat a luxurious look.

side edges of straps matching side edges of bib. Stitch through all thicknesses. Press lower raw edge of bib to outside. Lay waistband on lower edge of bib matching centre fronts. Stitch through all thicknesses.

9   Make 16 mm buttonholes at back end of each strap. Sew on buttons to correspond, approx. 5 cm in from centre back edges of skirt.

10 Sew side and crotch seams of bloomers. Press.

11 Sew lace around lower leg edges. Press seams towards fabric. Edgestitch to secure.

12 Zigzag 55 cm elastic around inside of each leg along marked line to form frills.

13 Turn in 5 mm at waist edge. Press. Turn in another 1 cm, press. Stitch down to form casing leaving small opening to insert elastic. Thread elastic through

casing. Join ends. Close opening.

14 Cut strips of fabric approximately 20 cm x 6 cm. Fold strips over double lengthways and roll up to form fabric roses. To decorate Eloise's hat, glue on these roses and artificial flowers. Make a bow out of fabric and attach to hat.

✂ **H I N T** ✂

Use craft glue as a quick and easy alternative to sewing in many areas of toy making and especially for trimming.

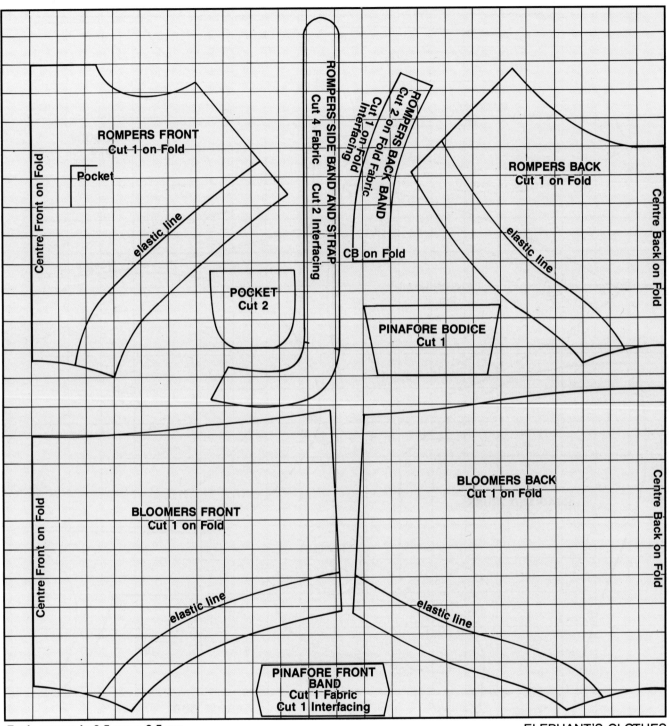

ROMPERS FRONT
Cut 1 on Fold

Pocket

Centre Front on Fold

elastic line

ROMPERS SIDE BAND AND STRAP
Cut 4 Fabric   Cut 2 Interfacing

ROMPERS BACK BAND
Cut 2 on Fold Fabric
Cut 1 on Fold Interfacing

CB on Fold

ROMPERS BACK
Cut 1 on Fold

elastic line

Centre Back on Fold

POCKET
Cut 2

PINAFORE BODICE
Cut 1

BLOOMERS FRONT
Cut 1 on Fold

Centre Front on Fold

elastic line

BLOOMERS BACK
Cut 1 on Fold

elastic line

Centre Back on Fold

PINAFORE FRONT
BAND
Cut 1 Fabric
Cut 1 Interfacing

Each square is 2.5 cm x 2.5 cm.

ELEPHANT'S CLOTHES

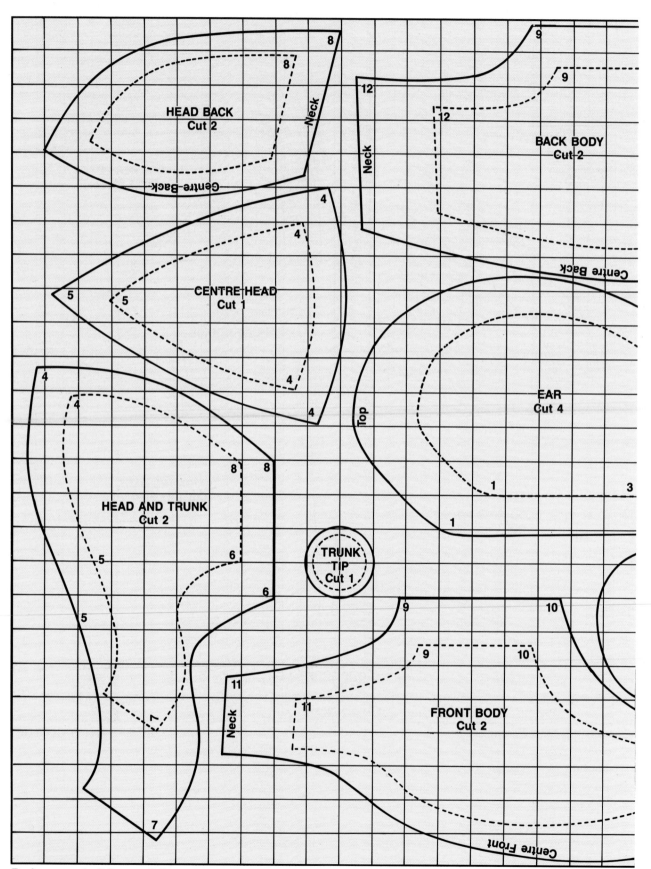

Each square is 2.5 cm x 2.5 cm.

Some pattern pieces have been divided to fit. After tracing, tape adjoining edges together without overlapping.

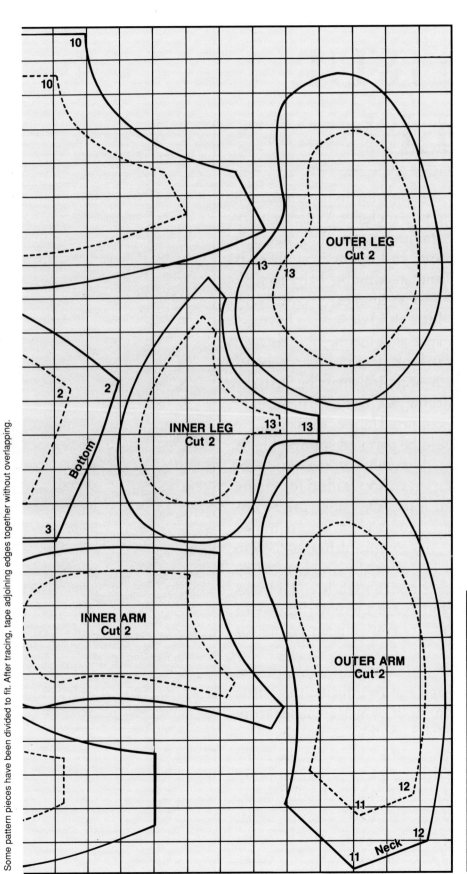

Some pattern pieces have been divided to fit. After tracing, tape adjoining edges together without overlapping.

10
10
OUTER LEG
Cut 2
13 13
2 2
INNER LEG
Cut 2
13 13
Bottom
3
INNER ARM
Cut 2
OUTER ARM
Cut 2
12
11
11 Neck 12

ELOISE AND BABY ROSE ELEPHANT

✂ H I N T ✂

Keep your soft toys in good repair. Mend any damage as soon as you become aware of it. Most toys are able to be salvaged in this way saving much sadness when a dearly loved friend falls apart.

OH, YOU BEAUTIFUL DOLL!

ix delightful dolls to make and dress include Annie, a very traditional rag doll, her soft and cuddly nursery friends and an adorable baby to tuck into its own carry cot. Every little child dreams of having a special someone of their own to look after and share secrets. A soft doll may be just the thing. We have used plain, light coloured fabrics to make these lovely   dolls. Ideally, they should be soft and spongeable. A smooth finish fabric can be painted or embroidered quite successfully. Cream calico or homespun cotton is ideal for giving a doll that traditional, heirloom look. We chose pretty co-ordinating cotton print fabric for their dresses, lavishly trimmed with ribbons and lace. You may prefer a quite different look in primary brights and bold prints. For our baby doll in its carry cot we have only suggested a lace trimmed nightie and it looks perfect. Remember that dolls' clothes are a wonderful way of utilising that box of pretty remnants you've been saving for just such a purpose.

Traditionally dolls to be cuddled are not stuffed too firmly. They must be pleasant to hold and not too difficult for little hands to dress. The nursery rhyme dolls, which are made from felt, require firmer stuffing to give them the desired shape.

Experiment with pencil and paper until you find the facial expression you like then embroider the features in fine cotton or, for that special touch, silk thread. Many small stitches are better than a few large ones to give a delicate effect and will last much longer. Features can be painted on. Where there is a hat you need only to suggest the presence of hair with a few curls. Take care to secure the hair to the doll in several places.

Annie, a rag doll

Childhood wouldn't be childhood without a traditional rag doll to dress in all her finery – pantaloons, dress, pinafore and shoes. A beautiful rag doll is a perfect present for young children and is also a wonderful raffle prize for the annual fete or fair. The lovely clothes are sure to be firm favourites for dressing other dolls.

We designed this doll to have a rather mischievous face as she seemed to us to love playing tricks and hiding under beds. Experiment with pencil and paper until you find just the right facial expression.

DIMENSIONS
57 cm tall

MATERIALS
Doll: 30 cm of 115 cm wide light calico.
Hair: two 50 g balls of 8 ply yellow knitting yarn; narrow ribbon.
Dress: 30 cm of 115 cm wide cotton fabric; 1.6 m lace for trimming; 3 small buttons.
Pinafore: 30 cm of 115 cm wide cotton fabric; 3.10 m lace for trimming.
Pantaloons: 20 cm of 115 cm wide cotton fabric; 1.6 m lace for trimming. To achieve the desired effect try to choose co-ordinating colours and small prints in your fabrics.

Sewing thread; 7 mm wide elastic; felt for shoes; embroidery thread or fabric pens in appropriate colours for decorating face; polyester fibre for stuffing.

PATTERN
Cut pattern pieces out as directed. 1 cm seam allowance must be added around all pattern pieces.
Cut to size: pinafore skirt 21 cm x 45 cm (cut 2); dress skirt 27 cm x 90 cm; neck frill for dress 6 cm x 50 cm.

STEP-BY-STEP
Clip all curved seam allowances for ease. Join all pieces together with right sides facing.

Rag Doll
1   Sew darts in toes using a 5 mm seam. Sew leg sections together leaving top edges open. Turn right side out.

Stuff firmly leaving top edge clear for stitching.
2   Sew arms in same manner as legs. Stitch across elbows by hand to create a 'joint'.
3   Sew darts in head sections. Sew back head sections together. Sew body sections together at centre front and centre back. With neck edges matching, sew head sections to body sections.
4   With raw edges matching, sew front head and body to back head and body from A around head and down to B. Turn. Stuff firmly leaving lower edges clear for stitching.
5   Flatten and pin legs so that seams are aligned. Fold in 1 cm at lower edges of body. Position open ends of legs 1 cm inside these folded edges. Hemstitch across lower body edge using thread doubled and fixing legs into place as you go. Pull threads slightly to give some fullness to body shape.

6   Turn in 1 cm at top edges of arms. Handsew arms to body at points marked, taking care to place seams of arms at Xs.

Hair

1   Cut two pieces of cardboard, one 8 cm x 20 cm for fringe and the other 30 cm x 60 cm for crown and plaits. Place cardboard rectangles so that long sides are horizontal. Secure lengths of adhesive tape horizontally across each rectangle with sticky side uppermost.
2   Wind yarn around cardboard, building up layer upon layer.
3   To complete fringe when desired thickness of yarn is achieved, place another strip of adhesive tape across yarn over previous strip. Crease cardboard and very carefully remove yarn. Holding taped yarn over a ruler, cut through yarn opposite tape. Place taped centre section of yarn along a strip of fabric 18 cm x 3 cm. Stitch through all thicknesses to secure yarn. Baste fabric strip across front of head, taking care not to catch yarn. Push yarn towards face and baste to hold.
4   To make crown and plaits, follow directions for fringe as far as 'cut through yarn opposite tape'. Place taped centre section of yarn along a strip of fabric 25 cm x 4 cm. Stitch through all thicknesses. Fold under one short end of fabric strip and place it at centre of fringe tape over stitching and with half yarn lying to either side. Hair for plaits overlaps sides of fringe. Stitch by hand along centre line fixing hair to head, finishing at nape of neck. Draw half hair to either side and plait. Finish plaits with ribbon bows.

Dress

1   Sew shoulder and side seams of front and back bodices.
2   Sew skirt centre back seam as far as symbol using a 2 cm seam.
3   Gather top edge of skirt and attach to lower edge of bodice.
4   Fold neck frill double with right sides facing. Sew short ends. Turn and press. Gather raw edges of frill. Pin gathered edge to neck of dress with right sides facing and keeping raw edges even.
5   Fold back facings to the outside over frill. Stitch across facings and around

neckline, catching frill as you go. Turn frill upwards and turn facings to inside. Press frill seam allowance towards dress. Edgestitch neck edge, catching seam allowances as you go.
6   Sew sleeve seams. Turn up 3.5 cm hem at lower edge of sleeves. Stitch again 1 cm away to make casing for elastic. Thread elastic through casing. Secure ends.
7   Gather sleeve heads. Sew sleeves into armholes.
8   Turn up 1 cm hem at lower edge of dress. Sew lace around inside of hem.
9   Make buttonholes on left back as marked. Sew on buttons.

Pinafore

1   Place centre bodice and facing with right sides together. Sew around neck and centre back edges. Place side bodice pieces together in same way and stitch around armhole edges. Turn right side out. Press. With raw edges matching, stitch lace along centre seamline of side bodice sections.
2   Stitch lace along outside seamline of armhole frills (main fabric). Place frill facing pieces (contrast fabric) on frills, right sides together. Stitch along trimmed edge. Turn and press. Gather raw, curved edge. Pin gathered edge of frills to side bodice sections with raw edges even and main fabric facing upwards.
3   Sew centre front sections to side sections with right sides together, keeping raw edges even and stitching through all thicknesses.
4   Sew bodice side seams.
5   Round centre front and centre back corners of pinafore skirt sections.

Narrow hem front and lower edges of skirt sections. Trim with lace. Gather upper edges. Pin to bodice so that skirt sections meet at centre front and centre back. Stitch.
6   Make four 30 cm long ties from fabric scraps. Fold under one raw end of each tie. Stitch these folded ends to pinafore back at neck and waist. Knot other ends of ties. Tie into bows to secure pinafore.
7   Stitch heart-shaped pockets and facings together with right sides facing. Make a small slit in facing just above point of heart and turn pocket right side out through this hole. Press. Sew pockets on either side of centre front skirt as marked.

Pantaloons

1   With right sides facing, sew sections together at centre front and centre back. Note there are no side seams. Fold so that seams are aligned at centre and stitch inner leg seam continuously from ankle to ankle.
2   Turn in 1.5 cm at top edge. Stitch, forming casing. Thread elastic through casing and secure ends.
3   Turn up 3.5 cm hem at leg ends. Stitch lace around outside to secure hem. Stitch again 1 cm away to form casing. Stitch another row of lace 3 cm above casing. Thread elastic through casing. Secure ends.

Shoes

1   Stitch shoe sections together at centre back. Using straight stitch sew 5 mm in along upper edge. Trim felt back to near stitching. Sew a fine zigzag stitch over straight stitching and covering edge. Sew sections together at centre front.
2   Sew upper shoe sections to soles.
3   Zigzag all edges of two 1 cm x 20 cm strips of felt. Tie into bows and attach to shoes.

SHOE SOLE
Cut 2

Front

grain

PINAFORE SIDE BODICE
Cut 4

Back

Centre

Centre Front on Fold

DRESS
FRONT BODICE
Cut 1 on Fold

• button

• button

Foldline

DRESS BACK BODICE
Cut 2

• button

grain

DRESS SLEEVE
Cut 2

elastic line

Some pattern pieces have been divided to fit. After tracing, tape adjoining edges together without overlapping.

Each square is 2.5 cm x 2.5 cm.   Add 1cm seam allowance around all pattern pieces.

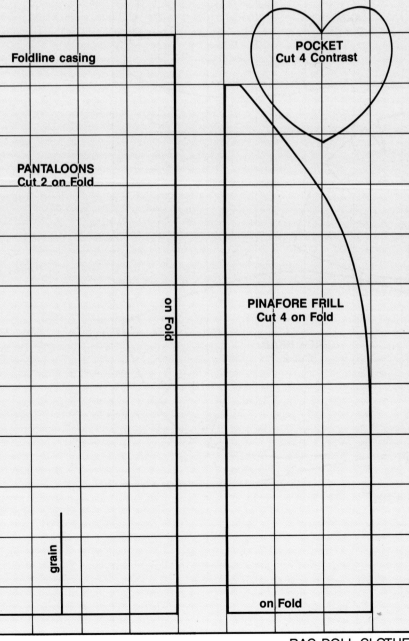

SHOE Cut 4

Front on Fold

Centre BACK

PINAFORE CENTRE BODICE
Cut 2 on Fold

Foldline casing

POCKET
Cut 4 Contrast

PANTALOONS
Cut 2 on Fold

on Fold

PINAFORE FRILL
Cut 4 on Fold

grain

on Fold

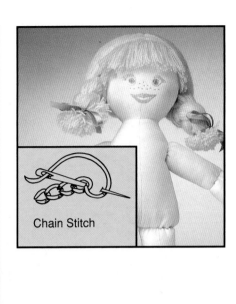

Chain Stitch

RAG DOLL CLOTHES

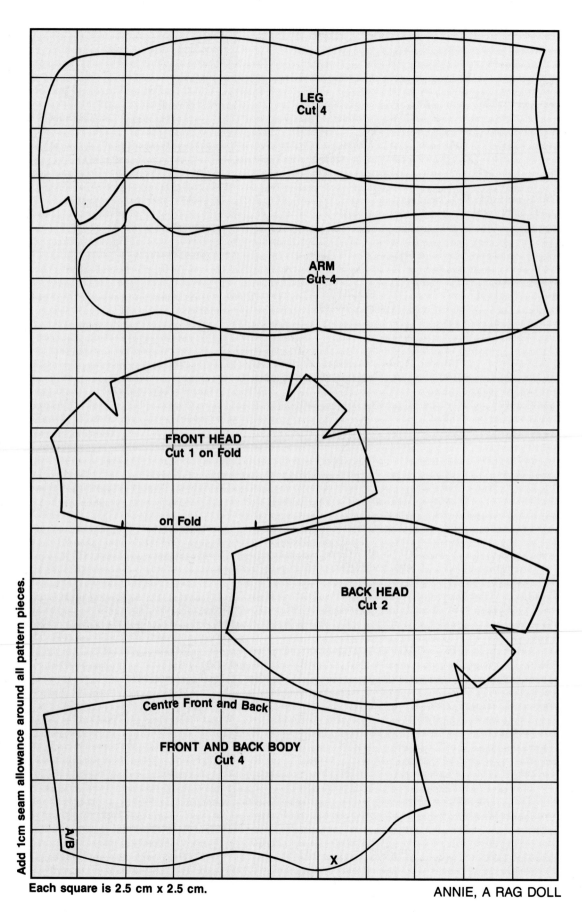

LEG
Cut 4

ARM
Cut 4

FRONT HEAD
Cut 1 on Fold

on Fold

BACK HEAD
Cut 2

Centre Front and Back

FRONT AND BACK BODY
Cut 4

A/B

X

Add 1cm seam allowance around all pattern pieces.

Each square is 2.5 cm x 2.5 cm.

ANNIE, A RAG DOLL

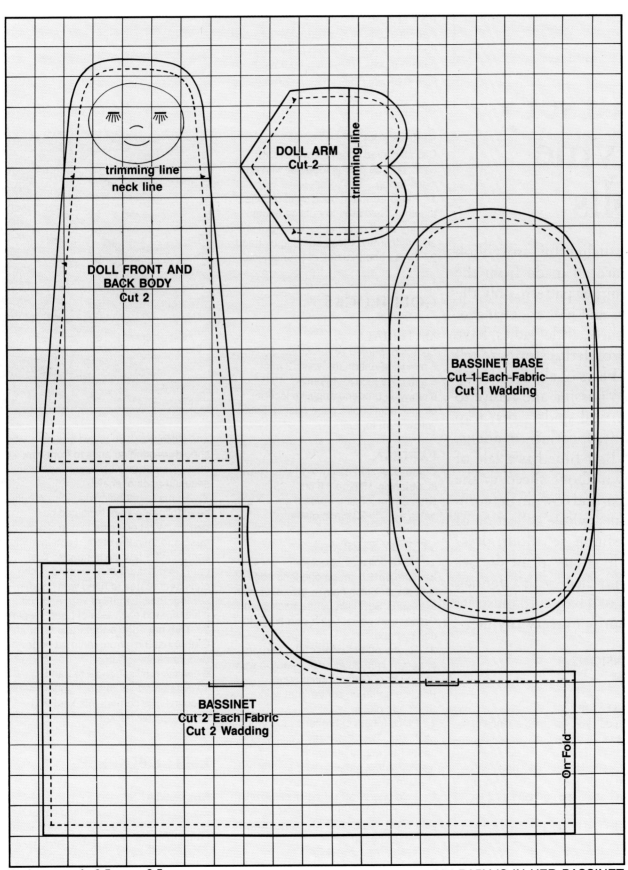

DOLL ARM
Cut 2

trimming line
neck line

DOLL FRONT AND
BACK BODY
Cut 2

BASSINET BASE
Cut 1 Each Fabric
Cut 1 Wadding

BASSINET
Cut 2 Each Fabric
Cut 2 Wadding

On Fold

Each square is 2.5 cm x 2.5 cm.

MY BABY IS IN HER BASSINET

Nursery rhyme dolls

These delightful storybook dolls are all made from the same simple pattern, only the clothes and hair are changed. Our three little ladies have such wonderful stories to tell about bears of all sizes, sheep that go missing and refuse to return, and spiders that leap on unsuspecting maidens. Little Boy Blue has a tale of his own about sheep in the meadow and cows in the corn.

Make a whole collection of these simple felt dolls, dress them in pretty print dresses and trim them with a bonnet, a bow or a basket to illustrate a favourite nursery rhyme.

DIMENSIONS
25 cm tall

MATERIALS
For each doll you will need a piece of felt 25 cm x 30 cm in a colour of your choice; small quantity of knitting yarn for hair; polyester fibre for stuffing; embroidery thread for decorating face; scraps of cotton print fabric and lace trim; narrow satin ribbon.

You will find materials required to clothe each doll in the special instructions for that doll.

PATTERN
Cut out one front and one back for each doll. 6 mm seam allowed around all pattern pieces. There are no pattern pieces for dolls' clothes. They are all made from cut to size pieces of fabric and lace.

STEP-BY-STEP
Clip all curved seam allowances for ease. Join all pieces together with right sides facing.
1 Place front and back doll sections together. Sew around outside edges, leaving small opening for turning. Turn and stuff firmly. Close opening by hand.
2 Dress and trim doll of your choice.

GOLDILOCKS

MATERIALS
Scraps of printed cotton fabric; 50 cm of 8 mm wide ribbon for waist; 2 m of 6 mm wide lace for trimming; 40 cm of 6 cm wide broderie anglaise lace for blouse; small doll's cane basket; bright yellow yarn for hair.

PATTERN
Cut to size: skirt 52 cm x 11 cm; shawl is a triangle 18 cm x 18 cm x 35 cm; sash 23 cm x 5 cm; apron 9 cm x 7 cm; hat is a circle 23 cm in diameter.

STEP-BY-STEP
1 Make doll as instructed.
2 Turn up 1.5 cm on one long edge of skirt piece. Stitch narrow lace over hem to secure. Sew skirt centre back seam. Gather skirt waist. Stitch skirt firmly to doll by hand.
3 Round off both lower front corners of apron. Trim outer edge of apron with narrow lace. Gather upper edge. Position apron on centre front skirt. Stitch into place.
4 Place length of broderie lace around each arm. Trim away any excess. Fold under raw edges and attach to arms by hand. Stitch a panel of lace across her chest from shoulder to shoulder.
5 Fold under raw edges of sash, crush slightly and place around waist, covering skirt waist and blouse raw edge. Sew into place by hand.
6 Fold in raw edges of shawl. Press

and stitch. Position shawl around shoulders bringing ends to front over sash. Tie narrow ribbon around waist securing ends of shawl.
7 To make her hair, wind yarn around head following lines indicated on pattern. Wind one side first to top of head and then the other. To help guide yarn, push a few glass-headed pins partly into head. When winding is complete secure hair to head with hand-sewing. Plait lengths of yarn and coil plaits around each side of head. Secure.
8 Trim hat edge with narrow lace. Gather hat 3 cm from trimmed edge. Secure hat over hair.
9 Stitch basket handle to hand.
10 Neaten edges of small square scrap of cotton. Tie corners into knot and place in picnic basket.

LITTLE BO-PEEP

MATERIALS
Scraps of three co-ordinating cotton print fabrics; scraps of 5 mm wide lace for trimming; 2 m pre-gathered 1.5 cm wide lace; 3 mm wide satin ribbon for

11 Sew on buttons.

12 Make shepherd's crook by twisting pipe cleaner into shape. Stitch to doll's wrist by hand.

LITTLE MISS MUFFET

MATERIALS

Scraps of cotton print fabric; scrap of co-ordinating plain fabric; 3.2 m of 7 mm wide lace; yarn for hair; 3 mm wide ribbon; three brown pipe cleaners.

PATTERN

6 mm seams allowed.

Cut to size: skirt 52 cm x 11 cm; hat is a circle 23 cm in diameter; shawl is two triangles each 15 cm x 28 cm x 28 cm; ruffles for skirt, hat and sleeves 2.80 m x 7 cm; sleeve 10 cm x 3.5 cm (cut 2).

STEP-BY-STEP

1 Make doll as instructed.

2 Press under top and lower raw edges of sleeves. Cut two 15 cm lengths of strip for ruffles. Press over double. Gather raw edges. Pin gathered edge under folded wrist edge of each sleeve. On outside, pin a length of lace over folded fabric edge. Stitch through all thicknesses, catching lace, fabric and ruffle as you go. Place completed sleeve over doll's arms. Close underarm seam by hand.

3 Cut 130 cm off ruffle strip. Fold over double. Gather raw edges.

4 Sew skirt centre back seam. Fold under raw edge of lower skirt. Position ruffle under folded edge. On outside, pin lace over folded fabric edge. Stitch through all thicknesses. Gather top edge of skirt. Stitch skirt securely around doll's waist.

5 Join shawl pieces together at 15 cm edge. Press under all raw edges of shawl. Stitch lace all around under folded edges. Position shawl around doll's shoulders so that ends cross over at front and are stitched together at centre back under shawl.

6 Make hair as for Little Bo-Peep.

7 Trim edge of hat as skirt hem with remaining ruffle fabric and lace. Gather 3.5 cm from trimmed edge of hat. Draw up gathers to fit doll's head. Stitch hat into place.

trims; three small pearl buttons; a pipe cleaner for shepherd's crook.

PATTERN

Cut two blouse pieces and four shoe pieces from doll pattern as shown. 6 mm seam allowed all around. Cut to size: peplum 13 cm x 6 cm (cut two); skirt 52 cm x 11 cm; shawl is a triangle 18 cm x 18 cm x 35 cm; sash 23 cm x 5 cm; hat is a circle 23 cm in diameter.

STEP-BY-STEP

1 Fold over and press neck and sleeve edges of blouse pieces. Neaten lower edges of blouse. Fold over and press ankle edges of shoe pieces. Placing a length of gathered lace under neck edges, pin one blouse piece and two shoe pieces into position on doll front and doll back. Stitch through all thicknesses.

2 Make doll as instructed, stitching blouse and shoes into place as you go.

3 Trim one long edge of skirt with gathered lace. Stitch centre back skirt seam. Gather upper edge of skirt. Attach skirt to doll by hand.

4 Round off lower corners of peplums. Trim lower edges with gathered lace. Gather upper edges. Place peplums on top of skirt so that they meet at centre front and centre back. Attach to skirt by hand.

5 Fold under and press raw edges of sash. Crush slightly and wrap around doll's waist. Handsew to secure.

6 Fold under raw edges of shawl. Stitch. Tie around doll's shoulders. Catch to doll with a few small stitches.

7 Tie bows of narrow ribbon around neck, wrists and ankles.

8 Wrap hair around doll's head as for Goldilocks. Make curls by winding yarn around fingers ten or twelve times. Slide off fingers and attach to sides of head and brow with small stitches. Make as many bunches of curls as you want to give desired effect.

9 Turn under raw edge of hat. Sew lace around edge. Gather 3.5 cm from edge. Draw up gathering to fit doll's head and stitch hat into place. Stitch small bow to centre back.

10 Embroider eyes, eyelashes and mouth. Indicate cheeks with pink powder blusher.

8 Trim ankles and hat with narrow ribbon bows.

9 Cut two pipe cleaners in half. Bend each piece into M shape. Place four Ms together. Fasten around middle with another pipe cleaner, winding its end around to look like spider's head. Attach spider to dangle from Miss Muffet's hat with sewing thread.

LITTLE BOY BLUE

MATERIALS

Remnant of fine cotton or voile; scrap of cotton print fabric for pants; 3 mm wide ribbon; embroidery thread; yarn for hair.

PATTERN

Cut two pieces for pants, using doll pattern from waist to feet. 6 mm seam allowed.

Cut to size: tunic side panels 25 cm x 17 cm (cut 2); sleeves 11 cm x 11 cm (cut 2); tunic centre panel 12 cm x 8 cm (cut 2); embroidered panels 5 cm x 5 cm (cut 2, unless you wish to have these doubled to facilitate embroidery in which case cut 4); embroidered sleeve bands 11 cm x 5 cm (cut 2); hat is a circle 23 cm in diameter (cut 2).

STEP-BY-STEP

1 Turn under raw edge at pants waist. Position pants on front and back of doll. Stitch pants across waist.

2 Make doll as instructed.

3 Fold side panels in half lengthways. Press. Mark centre of raw long edges.

4 Fold sleeve pieces in half so that folded edge is at wrist. Mark centre of raw edge opposite fold. Sew this raw edge to tunic side edge, matching centre markings.

5 Fold under 1 cm at top raw edge of tunic centre panels. Place side edges of centre panels under folded edges of side panels, matching hemlines. Stitch.

6 Gather top edges of centre panels 5 mm and 4 cm from top edge. Draw up gathering to be 3.5 cm wide.

7 With right sides facing and matching edges of underarms and side panels, stitch in a continuous seam from sleeve edge to hem.

8 Turn up hem and embroider pattern in cross stitch by hand or machine. Stitch lace around hem.

9 Decorate sleeve bands and front and back embroidered panels as hem.

10 Place tunic on doll. Gather tunic slightly across shoulders, stitching onto doll to secure. Sew sleeves to wrists, gathering sleeves as you go.

11 Turn in raw edges of embroidered inserts. Attach to front and back tunic, covering gathering.

12 Slightly gather sleeve underarm seams, stitching to doll to secure. Attach embroidered sleeve bands around sleeve ends.

13 Embroider face as shown.

14 To make hair, stitch centre of 10 cm lengths of yarn to 25 cm length of tape. Attach tape around head from back of neck, over ears and forehead and back to neck. Brush all hair forward and downwards. Trim hair only when hat is attached.

15 Place hat pieces together with right sides facing. Stitch around outside edge, leaving small opening for turning. Turn and press. Embroider edge as before. Gather around hat 3 cm from edge. Position hat over hair. Stitch to secure. Trim hair.

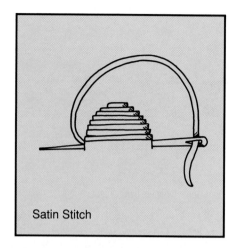

Satin Stitch

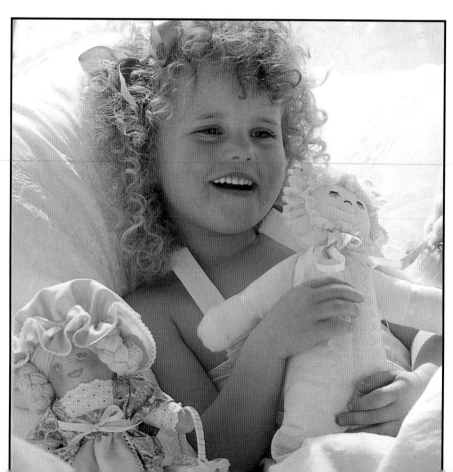

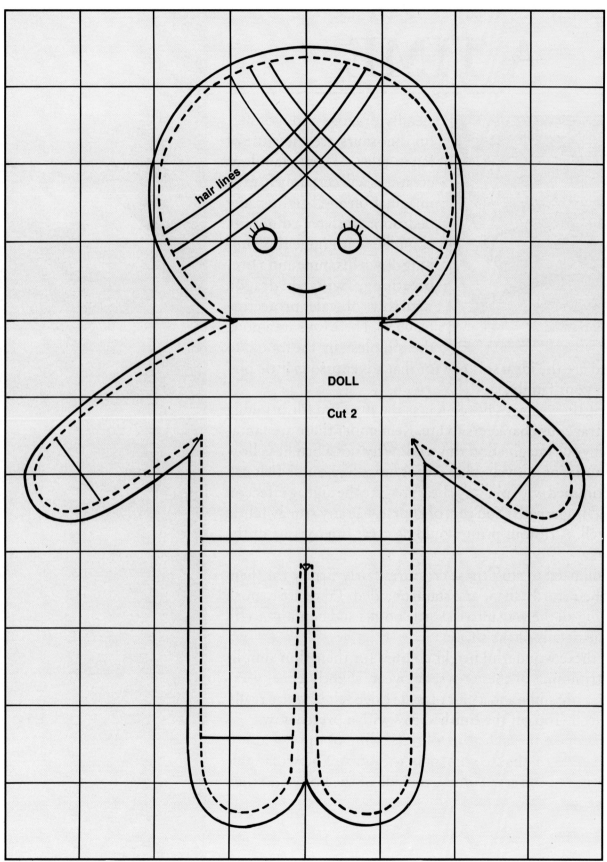

hair lines

DOLL

Cut 2

Each square is 2.5 cm x 2.5 cm.

NURSERY RHYME DOLLS

ONCE UPON A TIME

riendly dragons and wonderful dinosaurs are the stuff of fairy tales. These fabulous creatures will certainly fire the imagination and brighten any bedroom. We have a dinosaur, complete with huge fins running down his spine and a fire-breathing, winged dragon with rows of scales protecting his chest. These toys are among the simplest in the book to make and are the ideal soft toy for that adventurous little boy or girl in your family.

Once again we have chosen felt as the medium for bringing these outrageous characters to life. Remember these are fantasies so let your imagination run wild. Why not a bright yellow brontosaurus or a lovely blue stegosaurus like ours? Felt can also be trimmed with pinking shears to give the zigzag effect on scales and fingernails. You can, of course, use any sturdy fabric just as well. A riotous print would be great fun for one of the dinosaurs.

You will need to stuff these creatures fairly firmly for them to hold their sturdy shape and stand unaided. Take care to push the stuffing all the way into the little nooks and crannies to fill out all the details of the shape.

Using these wonderful bright colours for their skin simplifies the trimming of these toys. A sweet, slightly cheeky expression, a big smile and a pair of wide open felt eyes are really all you need. Top off the finished toy with a pretty bow.

There is one unusual feature of the sewing of the two dinosaurs and that is in the attachment of the limbs. You will notice that they have been sewn on the outside of the body and then topstitched.

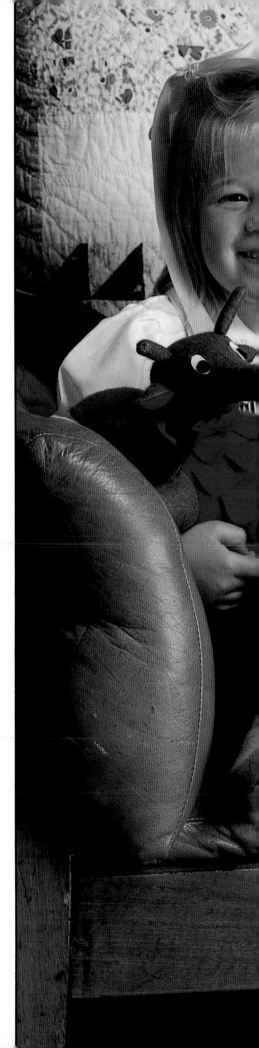

46

Belinda

Dinosaurs appeal to the imagination of children of all ages. With so many wonderful dinosaurs to choose from we looked for the all time favourites. A brontosaurus may seem rather unusual for a cuddly toy, but take a closer look at the beautiful Belinda. We think she is just the right shape to snuggle under a child's arm, listen to all the secrets and keep them secret like a best friend should.

We couldn't resist the wonderful bright blue felt for our Belinda, but let your imagination go with the fabulous range of felt colours available.

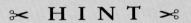

✂ H I N T ✂

Felt has no grain or nap, does not fray and stretches to mold into shape. Felt is not washable but it can be brushed gently or sponged lightly with a damp cloth.

DIMENSIONS
66 cm long

MATERIALS
45 cm felt; sewing thread; polyester fibre for stuffing; two small buttons for eyes; embroidery thread for decorating face; ribbon for trimming.

PATTERN
Cut pattern pieces out as directed. 6 mm seam allowed all around each pattern piece.

STEP-BY-STEP
Clip all curved seam allowances for ease. Join all pieces together with right sides facing except for upper legs.
1   Place back leg and front leg sections together. Stitch around all edges, leaving openings for turning as marked. Clip seam and turn. Flatten tops of legs and pin onto right sides of body sections between Xs. Attach legs to body using two rows of stitching.
2   Stitch body sections together all

around, leaving opening for turning. Clip seam. Turn.
3   Stuff body firmly. Close opening with a few stitches.
4   Stuff legs firmly, checking that Belinda stands balanced as you go. Close openings by hand.
5   Sew or glue on felt eyes.
6   Embroider mouth using chain stitch. Pull threads quite tightly from one side of head to other to contour face.
7   Tie bow around neck.

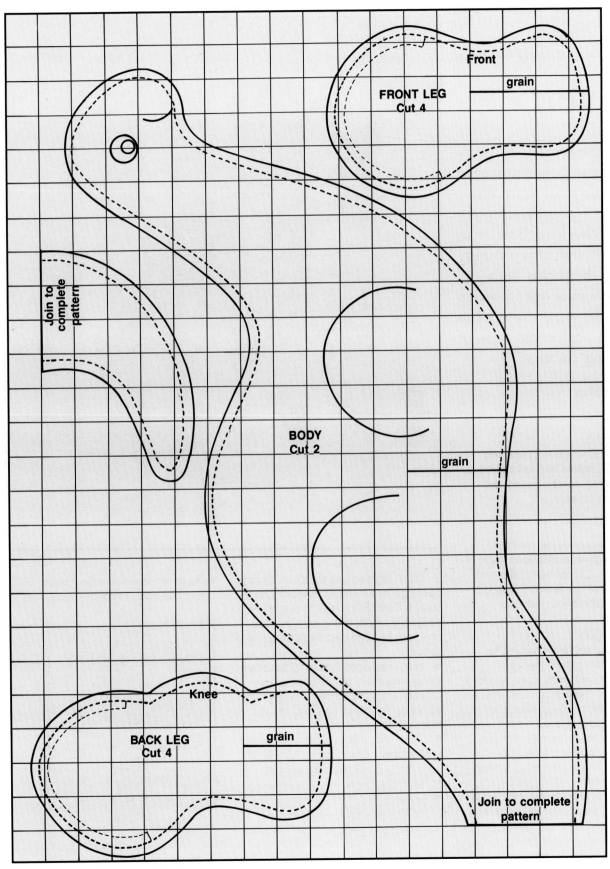

FRONT LEG
Cut 4

Front

grain

Join to complete pattern

BODY
Cut 2

grain

Knee

BACK LEG
Cut 4

grain

Join to complete
pattern

Each square is 2.5 cm x 2.5 cm.

Steven

Despite the armour of bony plates, the stegosaurus was in fact a gentle plant eating dinosaur. Our Steven is definitely a rather cheeky fellow who looks as though he is planning a raid on the flower beds.

The design is one in which you can let your creativity run riot with scales and fins of contrasting colours.

DIMENSIONS
37 cm tall

MATERIALS
40 cm red felt; scraps of yellow and purple felt for scales and nails; polyester fibre for stuffing; sewing thread; two small buttons for eyes.

PATTERN
Cut pattern pieces out as directed. 6 mm seam allowed all around each pattern piece. Cut out half scales and nails in each of yellow and purple felt. Scales are backed with red felt.

STEP-BY-STEP
Clip all curved seam allowances for ease. Join main pattern pieces together with right sides facing except for upper legs. Nails and scales are sewn with exposed seams using either straight or zigzag stitches.
1 Place contrasting scales together with red scales. Sew around curved edges. Trim with pinking shears. Stuff lightly with fibre.
2 Stitch nails together around curved edges. Trim seams with pinking shears. With raw edges matching, pin three nails to each leg.

3 Stitch leg sections together, leaving openings for turning as marked. Clip seams. Turn. Stitch legs to outside of body as marked, taking care to place one front and one back leg on each side of body.
4 With raw edges matching, pin scales along back seam of one body piece. Overlap scales as shown. Place smaller scales on head and near end of Steven's tail.
5 Stitch body pieces together all around, leaving opening for turning. Turn. Stuff body firmly. Close opening by hand.
6 Stuff legs firmly and close opening by hand.
7 Sew or glue on eyes. Embroider mouth using chain stitch. Pull threads

quite firmly from one side of head through to other to contour face.

✂ H I N T ✂

Always clip curved seam allowances. Shape is crucial for soft toys and an unclipped, curved seam will not allow for the intended curved shape to emerge.

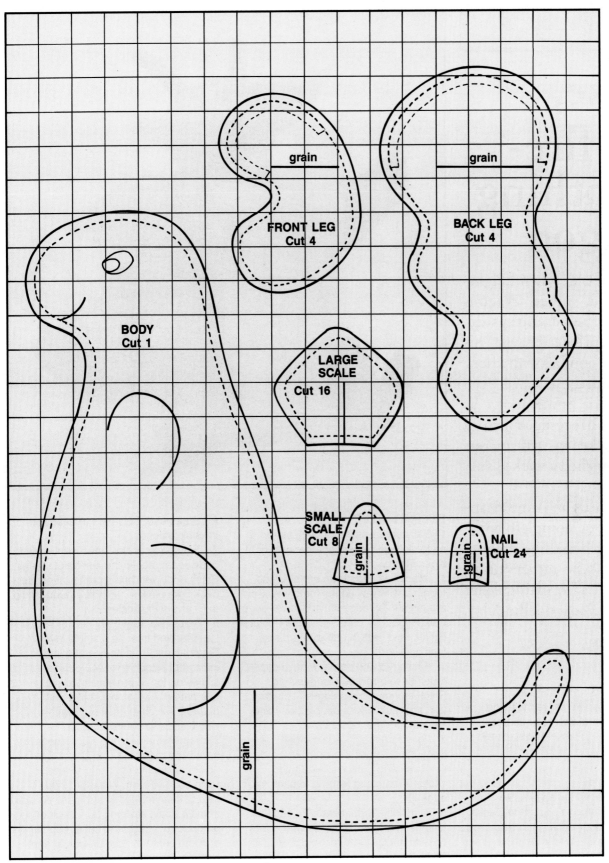

grain

FRONT LEG
Cut 4

grain

BACK LEG
Cut 4

BODY
Cut 1

LARGE
SCALE

Cut 16

SMALL
SCALE
Cut 8

grain

NAIL
Cut 24

grain

grain

Each square is 2.5 cm x 2.5 cm.

Spike, the fire-breathing dragon

In days of old, when knights were bold, fierce dragons roamed the countryside. Many a prince proved his courage in combat with a fiery foe. But dragons have been heroes too. Spike looks as though he has rescued many a damsel locked in castle turrets and vanquished a wicked sorcerer or two.

No 'once upon a time' chapter would be complete without its fire-breathing dragon. It may also be rather fun to make Spike a fire extinguisher from coloured modelling clay.

DIMENSIONS
25 cm tall

MATERIALS
30 cm green felt; 20 cm red felt; one purple felt square; polyester fibre for stuffing; scraps of white and black felt for eyes.

PATTERN
Cut pattern pieces out as directed. 1 cm seam allowed around all pattern pieces. Cut two front body sections to be placed together and treated as a single layer for added strength.

STEP-BY-STEP
Clip all curved seam allowances for ease. Join all pieces together with right sides facing.
1   Place red and green ear sections together with raw edges matching. Sew around curved edge leaving lower edge free. Repeat for other ear. Turn and stuff lightly. Fold ears in half with red side facing inwards.
2   Place red and purple wing sections together with raw edges matching. Stitch around curved edge. Clip seam, turn and stuff. Close opening by hand. Repeat for other wing.
3   Sew side head sections together from point of nose J to neck K.
4   Sew head gusset to side head sections matching J and L at back neck edge.
5   Cut 'flame' from scrap. Fold in half lengthways. Make a dart in centre front nose to enclose straight end of 'flame'. Stitch.

6   Stuff head. Sew ears to head with invisible stitches.
7   Pin spikey scales down centre back body seam, beginning just below wings. Stitch body sections together at centre back from neck to tail and around tail tip to B, enclosing scales.
8   Place two front body sections together and treat as a single layer. Stitch across front body along lines indicated. Attach a row of rounded scales on top of previous stitching, alternating rows of two scales with rows of three. Finish at neck edge with a single scale at centre front.
9   Join inside arm and leg sections to front body matching C to D and E to F.
10 Pin spikes to right side of feet on main body section. With right sides facing, sew front body and base section to main body, stitching from neck edge around arms, legs and base. Clip curves and into corners. Turn dragon to right side. Stuff firmly.

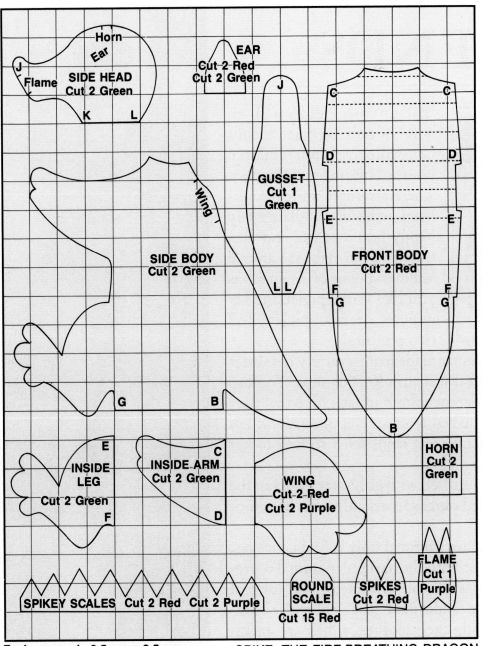

Horn
Ear
Flame
SIDE HEAD
Cut 2 Green
K L
J

EAR
Cut 2 Red
Cut 2 Green
J

C C
D D
GUSSET
Cut 1
Green
E E

Wing

SIDE BODY
Cut 2 Green

FRONT BODY
Cut 2 Red

L L
F
G
F
G

G   B

B

E
**INSIDE
LEG**
Cut 2 Green
F

C
INSIDE ARM
Cut 2 Green
D

WING
Cut 2 Red
Cut 2 Purple

HORN
Cut 2
Green

SPIKEY SCALES Cut 2 Red   Cut 2 Purple

**ROUND
SCALE**
Cut 15 Red

SPIKES
Cut 2 Red

FLAME
Cut 1
Purple

Each square is 2.5 cm x 2.5 cm.

SPIKE, THE FIRE-BREATHING DRAGON

HINT

Always double stitch tight corners and pressure points. It is very sad when a favourite toy comes apart.

11 Sew head to neck by hand. Sew on wings with purple side uppermost. Roll felt for horns tightly. Secure with hand-sewing. Attach to head at markings.
12 Sew or glue on eyes. Cut three narrow strips of red felt. Plait and tie around neck.

ANIMAL FRIENDS

These soft and cuddly animals will not only be great friends but will give your children hours of fun and creative play. There are three animal families which will stimulate many happy hours of fun and fantasy. You can make the animal families as big or as small as you like – one piglet and six puppies or four piglets and two puppies!

These farmyard favourites are made from a variety of fabrics from felt to a cheeky polka dot cotton for the pups. You can make each of the pups a different colour or pattern so that they can be named and distinguished from one another. Pink felt seemed just right for Hyacinth and lends itself so well to her cuddly curves.

The animals have all been stuffed with polyester fibre but the mouse family could be filled quite successfully with kapok or foam crumbs if you prefer.

The pig and dog families are trimmed only to indicate eyes, nose and mouth in character with the particular animal represented. The mouse family is lavishly trimmed, with each of them beautifully dressed in traditional garb. There are complete instructions for making their clothes, which are amazingly simple to sew. You will be rewarded for the effort with a trio sure to win any 'Best Dressed' award.

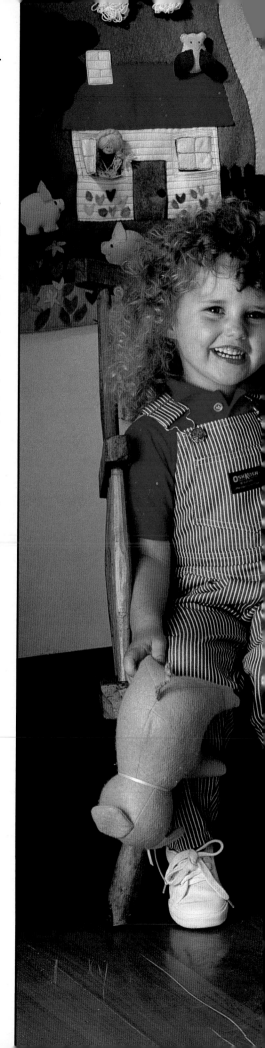

Hyacinth and her piglet

No storybook farm is complete without a pig and a piglet. We made two pretty pink pigs – Hyacinth and her piglet. Perhaps you would like to make two more piglets so that your family can enjoy acting out the Three Little Pigs or 'This little pig went to market'. Hyacinth and her piglet are sure to be top of the pops in your family. It is very simple to make the curly tail and dainty trotters. We chose pink for our porky pair but explore the other pretty felt colours for your farmyard.

DIMENSIONS
Hyacinth: 25 cm tall; Piglet: 14 cm tall

MATERIALS
30 cm pink felt for Hyacinth and 20 cm pink felt for her piglet; embroidery thread; scraps of brown velvet for feet; 10 cm elastic for each pig; two button eyes for each pig; polyester fibre for stuffing; sewing thread.

PATTERN
Both pigs are made following the same instructions but in different sizes. Cut out pattern pieces as directed. 1 cm seam allowed around all pattern pieces. Cut feet from brown felt.

STEP-BY-STEP
Clip all curved seam allowances for ease. Join all pieces together with right sides facing.

1   Join feet to leg sections of side and underbody pieces, matching points C–D and E–F.

2   Sew darts in side head pieces.

3   Sew head gusset to side head sections, stitching from G to H. Sew chin seam from J to K. Clip into seam allowance around nose area of head. Sew snout to nose. Carefully turn head right side out.

4   Sew underbody pieces together from A to B, leaving an opening for turning.

5   Fold tail double lengthways. Place elastic inside tail with end of elastic even with top end of tail. Stitch across end (securing elastic) and down long side of tail. Note that stitching is on right side – do not turn tail. Pull elastic up to make tail curl and secure end. Cut off excess elastic.

6   Sew darts in side body pieces. Pin tail below darts, matching raw edges.

7   Sew body sections together from L to B, catching tail as you go.

8   Sew underbody to side body sections from A to C then D to E and F to B.

9   Flatten ends of legs so that C and D and E and F meet. Sew around V-shaped feet. Trim away excess fabric.

10 With head inside body and raw neck edges even, stitch head to body. To tilt head slightly, as illustrated, place point K 2 cm off centre before stitching.

11 Turn pig right side out, taking care to pull out trotters completely. Stuff pig firmly beginning at nose and working towards feet. Close opening by hand.

12 Place ear sections together. Sew around curved edge. Turn and press. Sew ears on at markings.

13 Shape eye sockets by stitching from one eye position, through head, to other side with strong thread. Pull up firmly. Sew on buttons for eyes very securely. Embroider nose as shown.

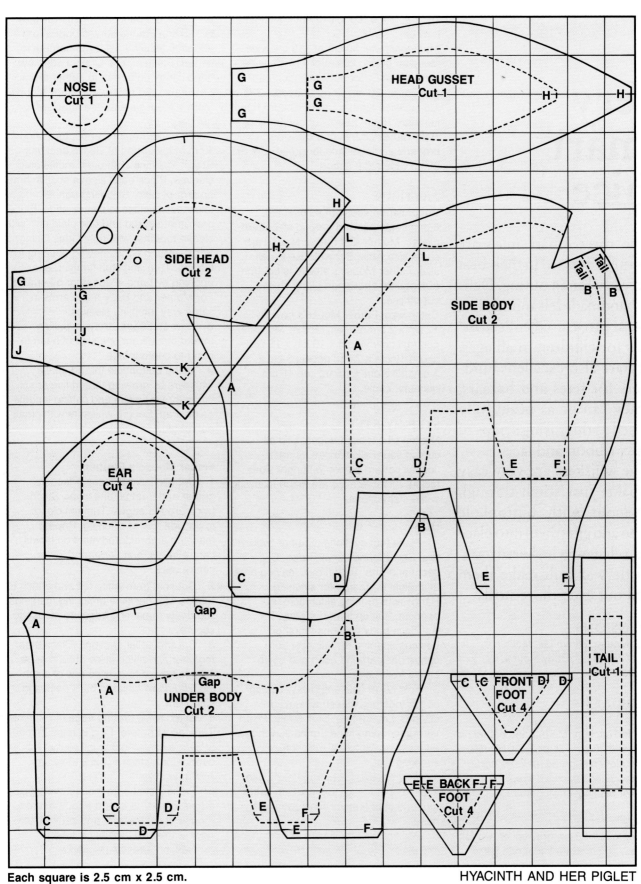

NOSE
Cut 1

HEAD GUSSET
Cut 1

G

G
G

G
G

H
H

H

L

SIDE HEAD
Cut 2

H

L

Tail
Tail
Tail

B
B

SIDE BODY
Cut 2

G
G

A

J

J

K

A

K

C

D

E

F

EAR
Cut 4

B

C

D

E

F

Gap

TAIL
Cut 1

A

B

A

Gap

C C FRONT
FOOT
Cut 4

D D

UNDER BODY
Cut 2

A

C

D

E

F

E E BACK F F
FOOT
Cut 4

C

D

E

F

Each square is 2.5 cm x 2.5 cm.

HYACINTH AND HER PIGLET

Very smart mice

These three smart mice are definitely dressed in their best and ready for an outing. Delicate handmade felt animals like these are treasured collectors' items for children of all ages. They are also excellent fundraisers for fetes and bazaars, as they can be as beautifully dressed as this, using scraps of fabric, ribbon and lace.

The whiskers are very easy to make. Just stitch through the snout with buttonhole thread and glue them into place for an elegant whiskered look. A little wax will make them stand out even more stiffly.

DIMENSIONS
Father Mouse: 25 cm tall; Mother Mouse: 25 cm tall; Baby Mouse: 15 cm tall

MATERIALS
Mice
30 cm felt each for Mother and Father Mouse and 20 cm felt for Baby Mouse; white buttonhole thread for whiskers; two small beads each for eyes; polyester stuffing; sewing thread.

Clothes
Father Mouse: 20 cm grey felt or two felt squares; 10 cm white felt or one felt square; piece red felt 12 cm x 2 cm for bow tie.
Mother Mouse: 30 cm of 115 cm wide fabric for dress; 20 cm of 115 cm wide contrast fabric for bow, frill, mob cap and apron; 20 cm string of beads; 3 m of 1.5 cm wide lace; scrap of lace for handkerchief; 15 cm narrow ribbon for cap.
Baby Mouse: 3.5 m of 6 cm wide broderie anglaise lace for dress; 1 m of 9 mm wide satin ribbon.

PATTERN
Cut pattern pieces out as directed. 6 mm seam allowed around all pattern pieces. Mother and Father Mouse are same size while Baby Mouse is half size. Father Mouse's sleeve is cut from arm pattern shortened along sleeve cut-off line.
Cut to size: Father Mouse's bow tie 12 cm x 2 cm red felt; Mother Mouse's contrast bow 90 cm x 10 cm x 12 cm; apron 10 cm x 7 cm; pocket 3 cm x 3 cm; frill 5 cm x 1.5 m; cap 15 cm diameter circle.

STEP-BY-STEP
Neaten all exposed edges. Clip all curved seam allowances for ease. Join all pattern pieces with right sides facing. All three mice are made following same instructions.

Mice
1 Place feet sections together two by two. Sew around curved edge. Clip seam and turn. Stuff firmly, leaving area at straight edge free for stitching. Handsew a running stitch across opening. Pull up thread slightly.
2 Place body sections together. Leaving opening for tail, sew from centre back around nose and down centre front body.
3 Fold tail in half lengthways. Stitch edges together with small zigzag stitches. Do not turn. Stuff firmly. Insert tail into opening in centre back with raw edges even. Stitch over opening, securing tail.
4 Sew base to lower edge of mouse, leaving opening for turning. Clip seam, turn and stuff firmly. Close opening by hand.
5 Position feet as shown and handsew into place.
6 Place ear sections together two by two. Stitch around curved edge. Turn and stuff lightly. Fold lower corners to centre. Stitch across straight edge by hand. Draw up thread to gather slightly. Sew ears onto Father and Baby Mouse. Mother Mouse's ears are attached to her cap.
7 To make Father's arms, turn under 1 cm at lower end of sleeve sections. Stitch. Machine embroider motifs onto sleeves. Place each sleeve section onto an arm section. Stitch through all thicknesses close to sleeve ends. Place one embroidered and one plain arm with sleeve together with right sides facing. Stitch around edge, leaving opening for turning. Turn and stuff firmly. Close opening by hand. Repeat for other arm. For Mother and Baby make arms in same way, omitting sleeves.
8 Sew on beads for eyes, pulling thread firmly from one side of head to other to contour face.
9 Using buttonhole thread, make whiskers by drawing thread five or six times through nose and cutting lengths as desired. Secure whiskers with small dab of glue.

Father Mouse's Clothes
1 Cut two jacket pieces. Place together and treat as one layer. Stitch twice around edges. Trim felt close to outside row of stitching. Repeat machine embroidered motif on lapels, centre fronts, and upper and lower centre back.
2 Cut shirt from white felt and attach to mouse with neckline matching markings. Handsew remaining edges to mouse to secure.
3 Cut two collar sections. Place them together and stitch twice around edge. Trim felt close to outside row of stitching. Handsew collar to back neck and shirt front.
4 Stitch twice around edge of red strip. Trim felt as before. Fold in ends to meet at centre back. Fold small strip of felt over centre, stitch at back to secure. Attach to collar.
5 Place jacket onto mouse overlapping edges slightly at centre front. Secure to mouse at centre front and centre back neck with small invisible stitches.
6 Sew on arms as marked.

Mother Mouse's Clothes

1   Sew lace to lower edge of ruffle. Gather ruffle and attach to lower edge of skirt.

2   To make apron, round off lower corners and trim lower edge with lace, gathering lace slightly at corners.

3   Fold in 5 mm around all raw edges of pocket. Press. Stitch onto apron. Tuck in scrap of lace for handkerchief. Baste apron to centre front skirt waist.

4   Gather upper edge of skirt and attach to lower edge of bodice. Trim upper edge of bodice with lace.

5   Put dress on mouse to sew centre back seam. Stitch centre back seam from neckline to hem. Secure dress to mouse at centre back bodice.

6   Fold fabric for bow with right sides facing. Stitch short ends and one long side, leaving opening for turning. Turn and press. Tie into bow. Attach to mouse at lower centre back bodice.

7   Trim lower edge of sleeves with lace. With right sides facing, sew under- arm sleeve seams. Gather curved sleeve heads. Slip sleeves onto arms

and baste to top of arms. Fold in upper edges and stitch arms securely to mouse, drawing thread through from one side of body to other.

8   Trim edge of cap fabric with lace. Run a gathering thread 2 cm in from fabric edge. Pull up threads and tie off. Stuff cap lightly.

9   Make fold between gathers of cap at sides. Pin ears into fold. On wrong side, stitch through all thicknesses, securing ears. Stitch cap to head. Attach small bow to centre front of cap.

10 Place beads around neck and secure at centre back.

Baby Mouse's Clothes

1   Cut 20 cm off lace for bodice. Cut remaining lace into two equal lengths. Place scalloped edge of one piece over raw edge of other. Stitch. Using scal- loped edge of lace as hem cut skirt to be 8 cm long at centre front, lengthening to 12 cm at centre back. Gather upper edge of skirt.

2   Place 20 cm of lace for bodice around mouse. Pin in fullness at centre

front. Stitch. Cut lace to fit, having 1 cm seam allowance at centre back.

3   Sew skirt to bodice.

4   Sew up centre back seam from hem to back neck.

5   Fold two 17 cm lengths of lace for sleeves with right sides facing. Stitch long sides. Turn. Gather sleeve heads. Slip sleeves over arms so that raw edges are matching. Turn in upper edge and stitch arms to mouse passing needle from one side of body through to other side.

6   Tie bows of narrow ribbon around waist, wrists and tail.

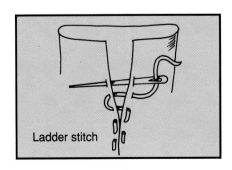

Ladder stitch

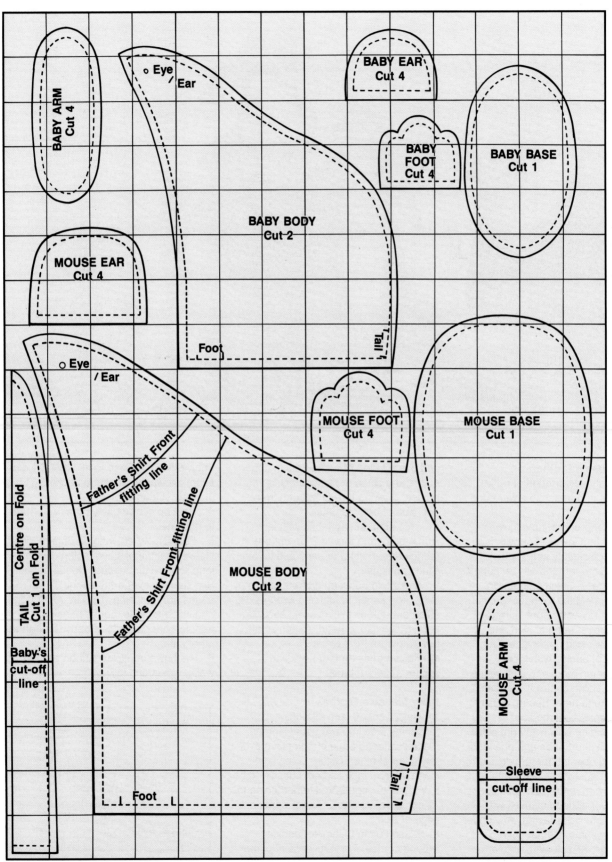

Each square is 2.5 cm x 2.5 cm.

VERY SMART MICE

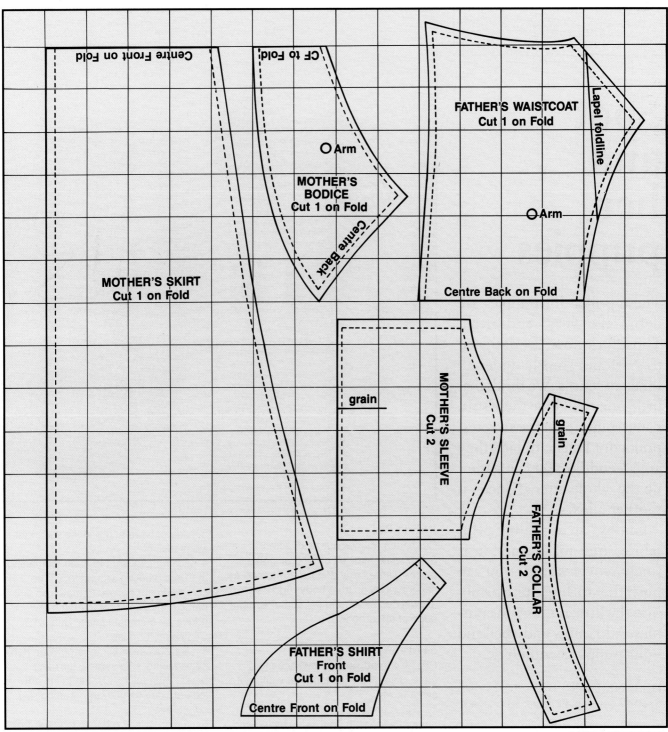

Centre Front on Fold

CF to Fold

○ Arm

**MOTHER'S
BODICE**
Cut 1 on Fold

Centre Back

FATHER'S WAISTCOAT
Cut 1 on Fold

Lapel foldline

○ Arm

Centre Back on Fold

MOTHER'S SKIRT
Cut 1 on Fold

grain

MOTHER'S SLEEVE
Cut 2

grain

FATHER'S COLLAR
Cut 2

FATHER'S SHIRT
Front
Cut 1 on Fold

Centre Front on Fold

Each square is 2.5 cm x 2.5 cm.

MICE CLOTHES

61

Spot and her puppies

These polka dot puppies are definitely very endearing. Those little noses are designed to sniff and snuffle under all kinds of fences. We think that little ones will love these soft, round puppies in the sweetest polka dot fabric. In fact, they are so cuddly you can gather up the whole litter at once – if mother allows.

Choose an appealing print fabric, but make sure it is finely woven so that you can push the stuffing quite firmly into the little nooks and crannies. Add a bow and a bell and your puppy is complete.

DIMENSIONS
Spot: 27 cm long; Puppies: 18 cm long

MATERIALS
50 cm of 115 cm wide fabric for Spot and 20 cm of 115 cm wide fabric for each puppy; polyester fibre for stuffing; scraps of black and white felt for eyes; sewing thread; ribbon for collar and bow; optional bell.

PATTERN
Cut pattern pieces out as directed.
6 mm seam allowed around all pattern pieces. Underbody and tail are traced as separate pieces from body. Add seam allowances all around tail and at straight edge of underbody.

STEP-BY-STEP
Clip all curved seam allowances for ease. Join all pieces together with right sides facing.
1   Stitch underbody pieces together at straight edge with right sides facing and leaving an opening between A and B. Press seam open.
2   With right sides facing sew body pieces to underbody, stitching from C around to D, taking care to sew right into corners. Clip seam for ease.
3   Sew ear pieces together around curved edge with right sides facing. Clip seam, turn and press. Pin ears to

outside of head at markings with right sides facing.
4   Pin head gusset to head, beginning at C and working around to E. The curves do not appear to match so it is particularly important to match raw edges for a smooth finish. Stitch. Clip seam for ease.
5   Sew tail sections together with right sides facing. Clip seams, turn and press. Stuff tail lightly. Pin tail to one side of body as marked, keeping raw edges even.
6   Finish stitching backs together from E to D, attaching tail as you go.
7   Turn complete body right side out. Stuff, beginning at feet and nose and working back towards opening. Close opening by hand.
8   Attach felt nose and eyes either by handsewing or with glue.
9   Decorate with ribbon collar. If desired, attach bell to bow.

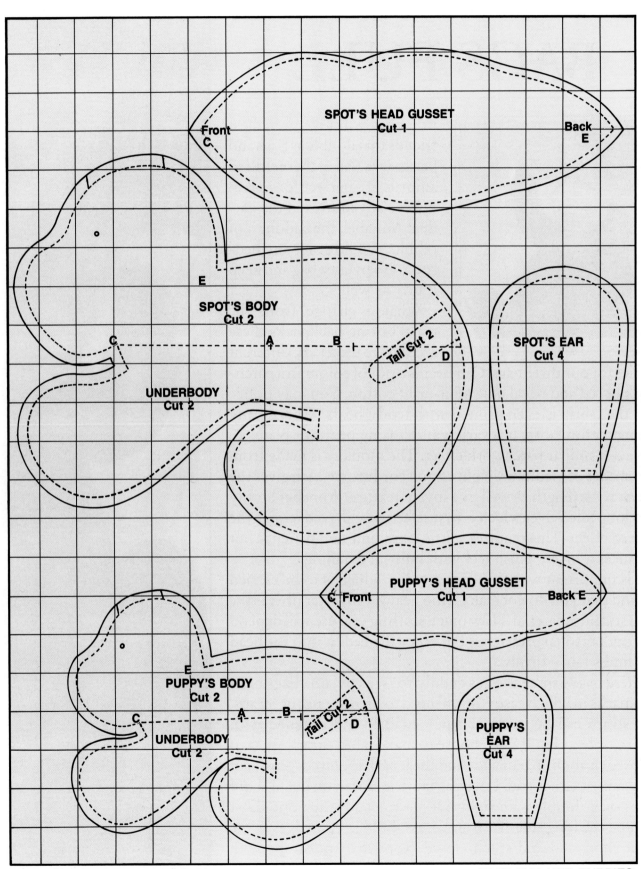

SPOT'S HEAD GUSSET
Cut 1

Front
C

Back
E

E

SPOT'S BODY
Cut 2

C

A

B

Tail Cut 2

D

SPOT'S EAR
Cut 4

UNDERBODY
Cut 2

PUPPY'S HEAD GUSSET
Cut 1

C Front

Back E

E

PUPPY'S BODY
Cut 2

C

A

B

Tail Cut 2

D

UNDERBODY
Cut 2

PUPPY'S
EAR
Cut 4

Each square is 2.5 cm x 2.5 cm.

SPOT AND HER PUPPIES

THREE BAGS FULL

ittle ones will love these best friends that double as bags and backpacks. All of these stuffed animals are perfect for make-believe adventures in the garden. Annabel, the cuddliest of rabbits, would grace any bedroom as a pyjama bag and keep it tidy as well!

What a change from the usual boring backpacks these are! We've used very different fabrics for our three bags. Our bear is a riot of colour in a patchwork of red and royal blue mini-print cotton. You may notice that the fabric is even printed with teddy bears! Choose any strong cotton fabric in a variety of pleasing prints or plains to achieve a similar patchwork effect. The monkey is made from two shades of medium weight cotton corduroy which gives the necessary strength as well as a lovely texture. Annabel bunny uses long pile velvet which is first selectively shaved to give the desired effect. This requires a little extra time and patience but produces a lovely plush feel with built-in detailing.

It is important when stuffing any toy which is to be carried around that you do not make it too heavy. Polyester fibre is the ideal stuffing material. How much stuffing you use will depend on your personal preference but you will need to stuff the head and limbs fairly firmly.

These bags can be used as cuddly toys, as pyjama bags or as backpacks in which case you will need to provide strong straps. The straps can be made of tape or fabric and fastened with Velcro or buckles. If you choose to make fabric straps cut two strips each about 10 cm wide and the length required, plus 1 cm for seams at either end. Interface fabric before you begin. Fold strips over double with right sides facing and stitch one short end and the long side. Turn and press. Fold in raw edges at the other short end and stitch closed. Topstitch the straps with several rows of stitching for extra strength.

Teddy backpack

DIMENSIONS
58 cm long

MATERIALS
You will need to make up about 70 cm of 115 cm wide patchwork fabric or purchase a similar quantity of mock patchwork fabric; 30 cm of 115 cm wide cotton fabric for lining; 70 cm x 40 cm piece of wadding; 20 cm square of felt for feet and paws; 20 cm nylon zipper; two 13 mm black shank buttons for eyes; black embroidery thread for decorating face; four 22 mm flat buttons for attaching limbs; strong buttonhole thread; 15 mm wide ribbon for trimming; 150 cm strong tape for straps (or sufficient to give length required); polyester fibre for stuffing.

PATTERN
Cut out pattern pieces as directed in fabric, wadding and lining. 1 cm seam allowed around all pattern pieces.

STEP-BY-STEP
Clip all curved seam allowances for ease. Join all pieces together with right sides facing.

1   Place each wadding pattern piece between its corresponding fabric and lining pieces so that fabric and lining have wrong sides facing. Stitch all around each pattern piece through all thicknesses, 6 mm from edge. Neaten raw edges.

2   Sew body centre front seam, leaving 20 cm open for zipper. Insert zipper. Press seams.

3   Join front body to back body sections. Press seams.

4   Join centre back seam up to notch for head opening. Neck opening should be 9 cm. Press.

5   Make darts in both front head sections. Press. Sew head centre front and centre back seams.

6   Place pairs of ear pieces together. Sew around curved edges. Turn, press and stuff lightly. Sew raw edges together and stitch into place between notches.

7   Sew front head to back head. Stuff head firmly. Stitch along neck edge 1 cm from edge. Neaten raw edge.

8   Contour eye sockets by stitching with a strong thread, used doubled, from one eye socket through head across to other. Pull up threads tightly. Sew on buttons very securely.

9   Embroider nose and mouth as shown, using satin stitch for nose and straight stitch for mouth.

10 With right sides facing, join head to body along neck edge. Turn to right side through zipper opening.

11 Sew felt paws onto upper arm pieces as marked. Place upper and lower arm pieces together with right sides facing. Sew around edges, leaving openings in back for turning. Turn and stuff firmly. Close openings by hand.

12 Sew pairs of leg pieces together with right sides facing, leaving openings for turning. Stitch felt foot pieces to lining foot pieces, 6 mm from edge. Join to legs matching centre front and centre back notches. Turn and stuff firmly. Close openings by hand.

13 Pin legs and arms to body where indicated. Place a large button over pin and, stitching through button with very strong thread, attach limbs to body.

14 Measure length for a comfortable strap position. We attached our straps at an angle from base of Teddy's head to his bottom. Allow 2.5 cm at each end of straps for hems. Turn under 5 mm at each end of straps and then another 2 cm. Stitch. Attach straps firmly to Teddy backpack where marked.

15 Tie bow around neck.

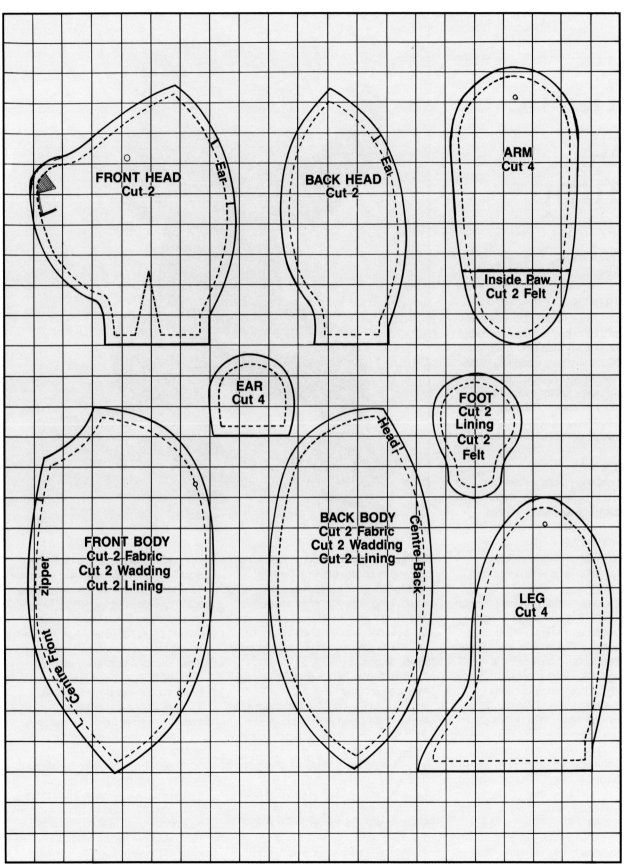

Each square is 2.5 cm x 2.5 cm.

TEDDY BACKPACK

Charlie the chimp

DIMENSIONS
49 cm long

MATERIALS
80 cm of 115 cm wide brown corduroy;
20 cm of 115 cm wide beige corduroy;
30 cm of 115 cm wide cotton fabric for
lining; 50 cm x 40 cm wadding; 20 cm
zipper; two brown 13 mm shank buttons;
scraps of beige felt for eyes; brown
embroidery thread for decorating face;
150 cm of strong tape for straps; strong
thread; polyester fibre for stuffing.

PATTERN
Cut out pattern pieces as directed from
fabric, wadding and lining. 1 cm seam
allowed around all pattern pieces.

STEP-BY-STEP
Clip all curved seam allowances for
ease. Join all pieces with right sides
facing.
1   Place each wadding piece between
its corresponding fabric and lining piece
so that fabric and lining have wrong
sides facing. Stitch around each pattern
piece through all thicknesses, 6 mm
from edge. Neaten raw edges.
2   Make darts on body sections
through all three layers. Press.
3   Place one body piece right side up.
Place one inside arm and one inside leg
on top of body piece, taking care to
choose arm and leg which point towards
front body. Matching circles as marked,
position arm and leg as you like. Sew
through all layers around circle. Repeat
for other side.
4   Place other arm pieces on those
attached to body so that right sides are

facing. Stitch around edge, leaving a 5
cm gap at centre back for turning.
5   Make legs in same manner as arms.
Join feet to legs matching centre front
and centre back notches.
6   Sew body centre back seam, leaving
20 cm opening for zipper. Insert zipper.
Press seams.
7   Sew centre front seam. Press. Sew
neck seam closed.
8   Fold tail over double with right sides
facing. Stitch long side to point. Turn.
Stuff lightly. Handsew in a neat circle to
body at symbol.
9   Join side head sections along seams
A and B.
10 Sew darts in upper face and both
muzzle sections. Join upper face to one
muzzle section from C to C, carefully
matching darts.
11 Join muzzle pieces along seam D.

Join completed face to side head
sections, carefully matching all points.
12 Place pairs of ear pieces together
with right sides facing. Stitch around
curved edge. Turn. Make a small
inverted pleat at notch in straight edge
of each ear. Stitch. Sew ears to back
head sections between notches,
stitching 6 mm from edge. Join back
head sections along seam C–B.
13 Sew front head to back head
matching centre front and centre back.
14 Gather neck edge slightly with
strong thread. Secure.
15 Contour eye sockets by stitching
with strong thread, used doubled, from
one eye socket through head to other.
Pull up tightly. Glue on felt eyes. Sew on
buttons very securely.
16 Embroider mouth as shown using
small chain stitches.

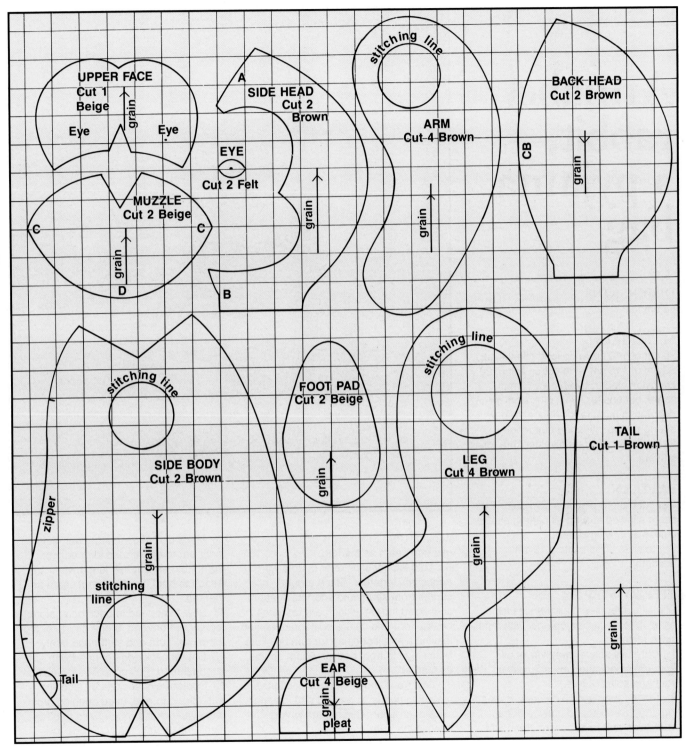

Each square is 2.5 cm x 2.5 cm.

CHARLIE THE CHIMP

17 Handsew head to body carefully matching centre fronts and centre back markings.

18 For method of attaching straps, follow instructions given for Teddy backpack.

Annabel rabbit, a pyjama bag

DIMENSIONS
66 cm tall

MATERIALS
70 cm of 140 cm wide long pile velvet; 30 cm of 115 cm wide cotton lining; 20 cm nylon zipper; two brown 13 mm shank buttons for eyes; pink wool for decorating face; fancy ribbon for bow; strong thread; stiffened buttonhole thread for whiskers; polyester fibre for stuffing.

PATTERN
Cut out pattern pieces as directed. 1 cm seam allowed around all pattern pieces unless otherwise stated.
Cut to size: tail is a circle 19 cm in diameter.

STEP-BY-STEP
Clip all curved seam allowances for ease. Join all pieces together with right sides facing.

1 Carefully shave away velvet pile from areas indicated on face, paws, ears and soles of feet.

2 Place fabric and lining body pieces together. Sew around outside 6 mm from edge and from now on treat as a single layer. Neaten raw edges.

3 Make darts in both back body sections. Sew centre back seam, leaving 20 cm open for zipper. Insert zipper. Press.

4 Sew centre front body seam.

5 Fold arm sections over double with right sides together. Sew around curved seam leaving an opening at paw for turning. Turn. Stitch arms to back body in 6 mm seam as marked.

6 Fold leg sections over double with right sides together. Stitch around curved front seam and short back seam. Join soles to feet taking care to match centre front and centre back notches and leaving a small opening for turning. Turn. Stitch legs to front body in 6 mm seams as marked.

7 Join front and back body sections, matching points all around and leaving neck edge open. Clip seams where necessary. Turn.

8 Gather neck edge with strong thread. Pull up tightly to close. Secure.

9 Make lower darts in head sections. Join head sections along centre front seam. Join top front head to back head, matching notches. Join back head to side back head sections along vertical seams.

10 Make dart in each inner ear. Join inner ear to ear around long edges. Turn. Fold ears in half lengthways. Attach to front head in 6 mm seam as marked.

11 Sew front head to back head along top edge, from end of one dart to end of the other. Turn and stuff head firmly.

12 Gather neck edge of head with strong thread. Pull up to close. Secure.

13 Contour eye sockets by stitching with strong thread, used doubled, from one eye socket through head to other side. Pull up very firmly. Shade eye sockets and shaved area of cheeks with pink powder blusher. Sew on buttons for eyes very securely.

14 Embroider nose with satin stitches and mouth with small chain stitches. Embroider heart on left front body with diagonal satin stitch, after first outlining shape in small backstitches.

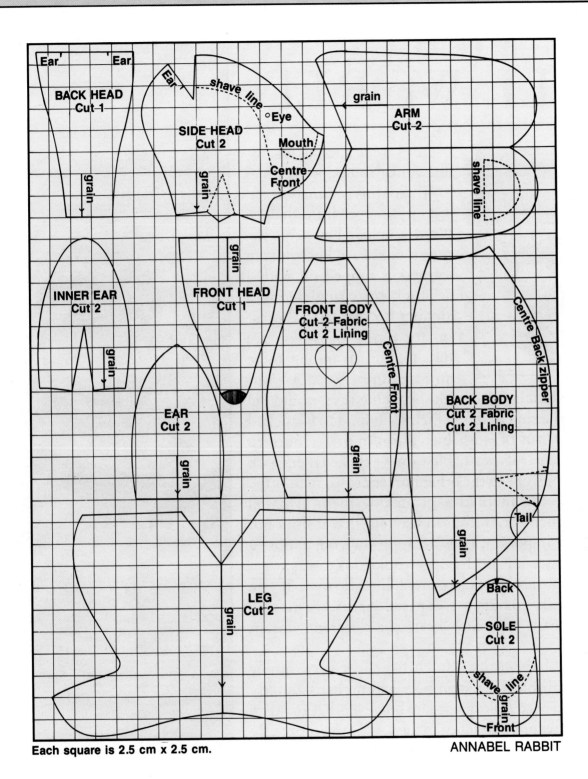

Each square is 2.5 cm x 2.5 cm.

ANNABEL RABBIT

15 Stiffen buttonhole thread with craft glue and allow to dry. Pull threads through face for whiskers.

16 Handsew head to body, matching centre front and centre back markings and extending seam to both shoulders to give added stability to head.

17 Stuff arms and legs firmly. Close openings by hand.

18 Gather around outside edge of tail with strong thread. Pull thread up to form ball. Stuff lightly. Attach to back body as marked.

19 Tie bow around neck.

20 If you want to make Annabel into a backpack attach straps as for Teddy backpack.

IT'S A SMALL, SMALL WORLD

irst toys are so special. Just for fun we made some pretty pram toys and tiny animals sized just right for little hands. We've included Coco, the cutest clown, whose lovely softness is topped off with a bell for baby to ring. If you're looking for that special present for a new baby you are sure to find it among these tiny treasures. What a wonderful gift a little basket filled with these cute toys would be!

We have made the clutch toys, which are bound to be tucked into little mouths, out of washable cotton in pretty nursery prints. To make them truly washable we have stuffed them with polyester fibre. For some of the other nursery toys, such as the teddies, we show the alternative of making them in pastel coloured felt. Remember, if you do use felt, that it does not wash. If this is an important consideration for you, choose a washable fabric instead. Timothy Bear would look just as sweet in a plain, pastel fabric embroidered with little flowers. If you prefer bright primary colours to soft pastel shades, try making the teddy bear chain with each bear in a different vibrant colour.

The trimming of these tiny clutch toys is a very simple matter. A little embroidery, a satin bow and perhaps a tinkly bell are all that you need. Take great care however that any trim you do use is very securely attached to the toy. This is especially true for little button eyes or bells. If you are at all uncertain leave them off altogether and substitute something else. Embroider the eyes and put the bell inside the toy.

Coco

DIMENSIONS
43 cm tall

MATERIALS
40 cm of 115 cm wide cotton fabric;
10 cm of 115 cm wide contrasting cotton
fabric for ruffle binding and underside of
shoes; pair of pink pantyhose or stock-
ings; white knitting yarn for hair; embroidery thread for decorating face and
buttons; polyester fibre; lightweight iron
on interfacing; small bell; 40 cm satin
ribbon for bows.

PATTERN
Cut out pattern pieces as directed. 6
mm seam allowed around all pattern
pieces.
Cut to size: upper ruffle 40 cm x 4 cm;
under ruffle 40 cm x 6 cm; 80 cm ruffle
binding.

STEP-BY-STEP
Clip all curved seam allowances for
ease.

1   Apply interfacing to wrong side
of hat piece. With right sides facing,
stitch centre back seam of hat. Turn
right side out.

2   Using two or three layers of
pantyhose fabric, cover a quantity of
polyester fibre and mould to form
a ball about 26 cm in circumference for
head. Try on hat and add or remove
stuffing as necessary. When satisfied
with size of head, stitch hose fabric
securely at closed neck.

3   Place body and leg sections together, matching raw edges and with
right sides facing. Stitch both from neck
edge to X at crotch. Fold so that seams
are on top of one another and stitch
ankle to crotch to ankle.

4   Bind one long edge of each ruffle.
Join ends of both ruffles. Gather
ruffles. Pin and baste upper ruffle onto
under ruffle.

5   Place upper and lower shoe sections
together with right sides facing. Stitch
around edges, leaving openings for
turning. Turn and stuff lightly. Close
opening by hand.

6   Gather neck edge of body slightly.
Place gathered ruffles around neckline.
Place neck into position. Adjust gathering to fit. Stitch head and ruffles to body
by hand.

7   Stuff body lightly. Gather around
ankles and draw up tightly. Securely
sew shoes to ankles by hand.

8   Make two small balls of polyester
fibre, covered with pantyhose fabric for
hands as for head.

9   Fold sleeve sections with right sides
facing. Stitch around edges, leaving
wrists open. Turn right side out and stuff
lightly. Gather around wrists. Tuck
hands into wrist openings. Pull up gathering tightly. Securely sew hands to
wrists.

10 Wind loops of yarn around fingers
ten or twelve times. Slide off fingers and
attach in bunches around edge of hat
with small stitches until entire edge is
covered. Stitch hat securely to head.
Attach bell to point of hat.

11 Embroider face as shown. Embroider
three buttons onto front of body using
small chain stitch. Tie satin bows around
ankles.

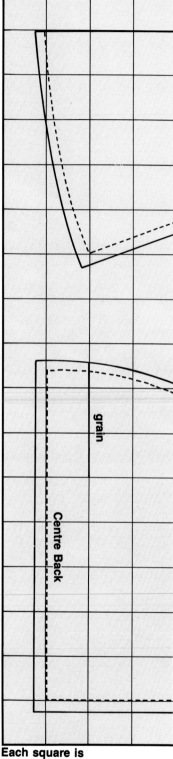

**Each square is
2.5 cm x 2.5 cm.**

Some pattern pieces have been divided to fit. After tracing, tape adjoining edges together without overlapping.

Teddy bear chain

DIMENSIONS

Each teddy bear: 13 cm tall; each heart: 4 cm across

MATERIALS

Scraps of felt 20 cm x 20 cm for each bear; scraps of cotton fabric 8 cm x 8 cm for hearts; 3 mm wide ribbon in desired lengths for trimming ends of chain and 15 cm for neck of each bear; embroidery thread for decorating face; polyester fibre for stuffing.

PATTERN

Cut out pattern pieces as directed. 5 mm seam allowed around all pattern pieces. Cut as many bears and hearts as you need for width of your pram or bassinet.

STEP-BY-STEP

Clip all curved seam allowances for ease. Join all pieces together with right sides facing.

1   Sew pairs of bear sections together, leaving small opening for turning. Reinforce corners with a second row of stitching. Turn pieces carefully. Clip seams. Stuff bears firmly. Close openings by hand.

2   Repeat process for hearts.

3   Embroider faces as shown. Tie bows around necks.

4   Handsew a heart between each bear. Begin and end chain with a bear. Stitch a length of ribbon at each end for attaching teddy bear chain to bassinet or pram.

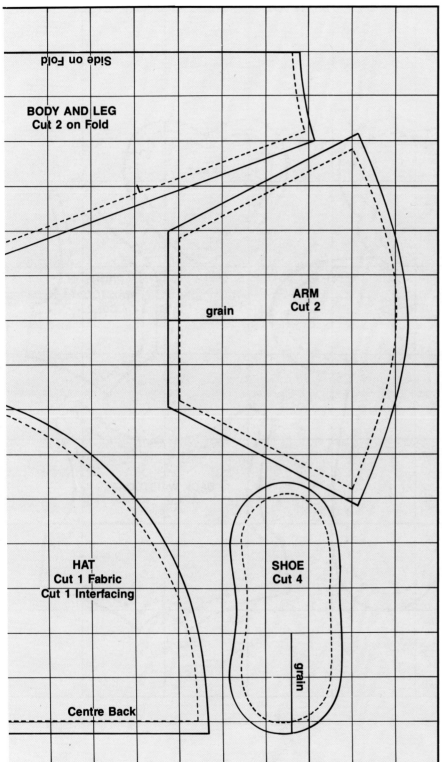

BODY AND LEG
Cut 2 on Fold

Side on Fold

grain

ARM
Cut 2

HAT
Cut 1 Fabric
Cut 1 Interfacing

SHOE
Cut 4

grain

Centre Back

Some pattern pieces have been divided to fit. After tracing, tape adjoining edges together without overlapping.

COCO, THE CUTEST CLOWN

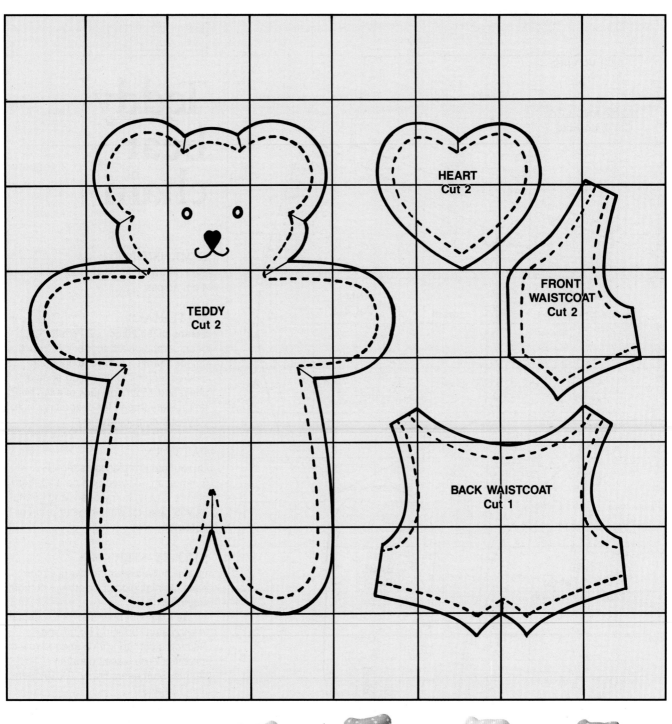

TEDDY
Cut 2

HEART
Cut 2

FRONT
WAISTCOAT
Cut 2

BACK WAISTCOAT
Cut 1

Teddies in vests

DIMENSIONS
13 cm tall

MATERIALS
Scrap of felt 20 cm x 20 cm and cotton fabric 8 cm x 8 cm for each bear; 15 cm of 3 mm wide satin ribbon; embroidery thread for decorating face; sewing thread; polyester fibre for stuffing.

PATTERN
Cut pattern pieces out as directed. 6 mm seam allowed around all pattern pieces. Cut one back and two front waistcoats for each bear.

STEP-BY-STEP
Clip all curved seam allowances for ease. Join all felt pieces together with tight zigzag stitching in exposed seams.
1   Place two front waistcoats on one bear section and one back waistcoat on the other. Stitch around waistcoat fronts, neck and lower edges along stitching line. Trim away excess fabric close to stitching. Using small satin stitch sew over original stitching covering raw edge. Press.
2   Place front and back bear sections together with right sides facing. Stitch around outside edge, leaving small opening for turning. Reinforce crotch and underarm area with an extra row of stitching. Clip seams for ease. Carefully turn right side out. Stuff firmly. Handsew opening.
3   Tie bow around neck. Embroider face as illustrated.

✂ H I N T ✂

Pressing of felt is not usually necessary. Felt is a natural wool fabric that tends to shrink if dampened or steamed. Should pressing be required, use a dry iron.

Bunnies in bows

DIMENSIONS
14 cm tall

MATERIALS
Remnant of cotton fabric 20 cm x 15 cm for each bunny; 60 cm of 3 mm wide satin ribbon; polyester fibre for stuffing; sewing thread; embroidery thread for decorating face.

PATTERN
Cut pattern pieces out as directed.
6 mm seam allowed around all pattern pieces.

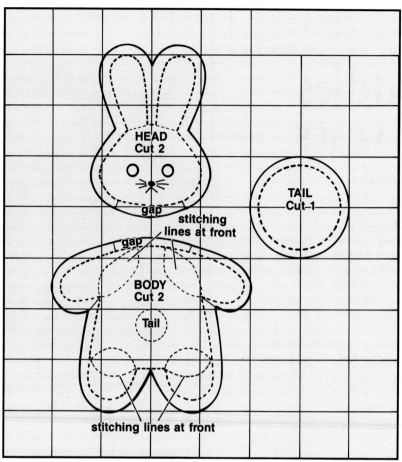

HEAD
Cut 2

TAIL
Cut 1

gap

stitching lines at front

gap

BODY
Cut 2

Tail

stitching lines at front

Each square is 2.5 cm x 2.5 cm.

BUNNIES IN BOWS

STEP-BY-STEP
Clip all curved seam allowances for ease. Join all pieces together with right sides facing.

1 Sew a gathering thread around tail piece. Draw up thread slightly. Stuff lightly. Draw up thread firmly. Handsew seam allowance to lie flat.

2 Place head sections together with right sides facing. Sew around edge, leaving opening at neck for turning. Reinforce area between and at sides of ears with another row of stitching.

3 Repeat above process for body sections, reinforcing crotch and under-arm area. Clip seams and turn carefully. Stuff very firmly.

4 Using ladder stitch, draw arms and body together along dotted lines.

5 Pin one end of ribbon to front neckline over one arm crease. Take ribbon down firmly around underarm, across back and around leg, through crotch and pin to tail position. Cut

ribbon. Repeat for other arm. Secure ribbon at neck and tail with handsewing.
6   Stitch tail into place with invisible stitches.
7   Sew head to neck and shoulders on outside with invisible stitches.
8   Fasten a length of ribbon around neck. Tie a small bow and fix to front.
9   Embroider face as shown.

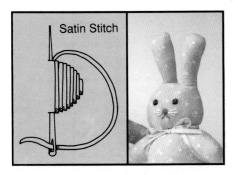

Timothy bear

DIMENSIONS
24 cm tall

MATERIALS
Piece of yellow felt 25 cm x 30 cm; embroidery thread in various colours; narrow satin ribbon for trimming; polyester stuffing.

PATTERN
Cut out pattern pieces as directed. 6 mm seam allowance allowed around all pattern pieces. Cut a neckline opening in one piece.

STEP-BY-STEP
Clip all curved seam allowances for ease. Join all felt pieces with tight zigzag stitching in exposed seams.
1   Place pairs of ear sections together. Stitch around curved edge and stuff lightly.
2   Place body sections together. Sew around all edges with small zigzag stitches. Stitch from crotch down to feet in straight stitching to define legs. Stuff firmly through neckline opening, beginning at feet and working up to head. Close opening by hand using ladder stitch, bringing head slightly forward. Attach underarms to sides of body with about 2 cm of handsewing.
3   Slightly gather lower edge of ears. Attach ears as marked.
4   Embroider face as illustrated. Define shape of waistcoat with chain stitch. Fill in waistcoat with flowers and leaves in lazy daisy stitch in a variety of colours. Embroider more flowers on ears, hands, head and feet.
5   Tie bow around neck.

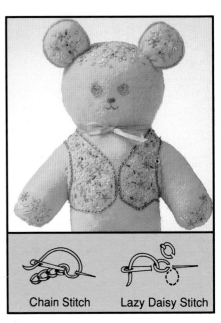

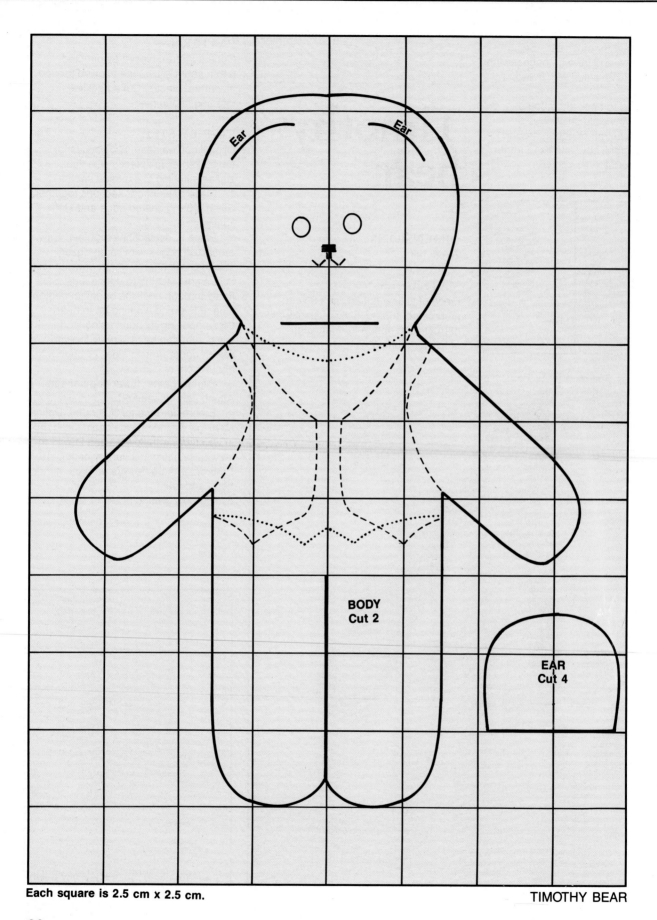

Ear

Ear

BODY
Cut 2

EAR
Cut 4

Each square is 2.5 cm x 2.5 cm.

TIMOTHY BEAR

80